Weigh-In

WEIGH-IN

the selling of a middleweight

FRASER SCOTT

THOMAS Y. CROWELL COMPANY
New York   Established 1834

PHOTO CREDITS

Photo section follows page 100.
The East Side Journal (Kirkland, Washington): page 1 (top left and top right), 2, 3 (top and bottom).
The Seattle Times: page 1 (bottom), 6 (top and bottom), 7 (top left, top right, and bottom), 8 (top left, top right, and bottom).

Manufactured in the United States of America

ISBN 0–690–00157–6

Library of Congress Cataloging in Publication Data
Scott, Fraser.
  Weigh-in; the selling of a middleweight.
  1. Scott, Fraser. 2. Boxing. I. Title.
GV1132.S524A38   796.8'3'0924 [B]   74–14882
ISBN 0–690–00157–6

1   2   3   4   5   6   7   8   9   10

This book is
for J. M.

I would like to express thanks to Nick Ellison, Jay Acton, and to Jack Scott, the Director of the Institute of Sports and Society. Each in their own way aided to write this book.

Contents

Weigh-In

1

DECEMBER 5, 1971

Luna Park Boxing Arena
Buenos Aires

THE AIR WAS SO THICK I could see it. It smacked of smoke and sweat and liniment that stuck to the insides of my nose. I listened as the crowd on either side of me chanted my name in rhythmic chorus. Then I sighed and let my eyes wander aimlessly. I tightened gauze-wrapped fists and shuffled nervously on my feet.

"C'mon," said Joe West bounding forward and up the steps that led to the elevated ring. He strained against the top rope, pushing it toward the lights, and sat on the middle one, pressing it to the canvas. He motioned me up with a twist of his head to the opening he'd made.

I followed his lead counting each step as I took it. One-two-three-four. It was like a dance, one that twenty-nine previous professional fights had committed to frightening memory. Tonight it promised to be a waltz of survival. I was going to fight Carlos Monzon, the middleweight champion of the world.

"Aw'right, get yerself loose," Joe West said.

I faced my tall and thin, black-skinned manager and nodded. I bounced up and down on my legs and threw three quick punches in the air. I turned to the crowd and let my hands drop.

My eyes fell on a swollen fat man who was stuffing his face with popcorn. He tossed it in, gulped, and then laughed heartily. From behind him came screams demanding things that no two men could give short of death.

"Over there," Joe West said. He pointed at a small box on the canvas in a neutral corner. In it were half a dozen golden chunks of resin. "Go an' step in it. It'll give yah some traction."

I walked over to it and began kicking and rubbing my feet into them. I heard the resin crunch and crackle beneath my boxing shoes. I held onto the ropes with outstretched arms and hands for balance, still gazing at the crowd.

I glanced down at the reporters, their fingers wrapped around pencils, poised on pads of paper. My eyes darted to the announcer. His hands were choking a large microphone. His sense of anticipation was keen, but it could not rival my own. The referee kept a trained eye on both Joe West and myself. Everyone just waited for the moment when they would become part of the scene.

"There are the T.V. cameras," Joe West said, nodding to the opposite side of the ring. They stood partially obscured by all of the smoke and haze. I glanced at them and then back to the crowd. The first couple of rows held the dignitaries, dressed to the hilt. Behind them were the people, my patrons, my antagonists. Then one by one they started standing. Row by row, section by section everyone strained forward. Ten thousand voices snowballed forward as one.

"Here comes Monzon," Joe West screamed.

I spun around as each person watched the dark aisle. A tall man emerged from out of the shadows and walked purposefully to the ring. He seemed indifferent to those that grabbed and clawed for a piece of him. When he reached the ring he didn't hesitate, he ascended his throne. Like a fuse winding its way to the bomb, when he stepped into that ring the building exploded.

I glared at him, not more than twenty feet away, but he ignored me. I spit on the canvas and ground it in with my shoe, repaying his imagined insult.

"Let's get these gloves on," Joe West said, dangling two wine-colored boxing gloves in front of me. He pushed them over my handwraps and fidgeted with the strings that would bind them to my wrists.

"Goddammit, gimme a hand here. These foreign gloves is aw'ways fucked up!" Joe cursed.

I looked at the glove and placed my index finger on the knot. Joe West wound the strings around and around, and then pulled them tight.

"Tape," he then said.

Our corner man handed him a large white roll of tape. He covered the strings to prevent them from coming undone. If he could have gotten away with leaving them uncovered he would have done so. But no referee worth his salt would permit such a tactic. A smart fighter would be rubbing the laces across his opponent's face in the first round.

"This guy'll be easier 'n Nino Benvenuti," Joe said, shooting a glance at Monzon as he finished preparing my second glove.

My thoughts drifted back eleven fights to when Benvenuti and I fought for his title. He wasn't easy, I remembered. I felt the need to explain that to Joe West.

"Yep, this guy's built fer yer style," Joe continued, again quickly glancing at Monzon.

I stared across the ring. Carlos Monzon leveled me with a dull stare. It was his wall to hide behind, disguising any real clues to his substance. He looked like a machine from where I stood, with powerful shoulders that glistened from a prefight sweat. His jackhammer hands dangled loosely at the end of long arms. Two thin legs stuck out of baggy trunks. Everything in Monzon looked as if it had been reduced to elemental considerations. Mental activity was blended with muscle in a marriage of instincts.

I kept staring at him as Joe West finished taping up the gloves and slapped them, signifying that he was done. I wondered what Carlos Monzon saw facing him across the ring. His defeat? His destruction?

"Here's yer mouthpiece," Joe said. He jammed it in my mouth and the taste of tobacco fingers remained on it. My jaws jockeyed it until it fit tight.

"How yah feelin'?" Joe asked.

What would he do if I had said "terrible"? I then bounced up and down on my feet. "Good," was all I said.

I scanned the crowd again, trying to find someone. If I could locate him, then at least one of the evening's questions would be answered.

"C'mon, get loose," Joe advised, watching Monzon cross his arms across his chest and pull them back. Monzon's movements were smooth and deliberate, executed with practiced ease, a routine he had spent a lifetime perfecting.

When a man grows up poor, he quickly discovers the boundaries of his world. Early on he recognizes the value of his fists. They become a gift, a talent, a ticket to escape. When a man lands a punch on another man he takes you seriously. But Monzon was not just another guy beating someone up, he was the champion.

"What yah lookin' for out there?" Joe West then asked. "C'mon, yah gotta get loose." He reached out to rub my shoulders and I pulled away, hunching them up and down.

What could I tell Joe? I was looking for a man who had introduced himself to me last week as I tried to train for this fight. He said things that I thought had gone out with the Wednesday night fights. In no uncertain terms he threatened my life. He had couched that threat on the point of a gun barrel.

Joe should have seen the difference in me. We had been on the road for three and a half years. He had worked the corners in all my fights. A man can watch another man change in that period of time. I saw Joe grow older every mile. He should have seen my fears take form progressively in Italy, Paris, and finally in South Africa. It was hard for me to forgive this oversight.

The referee then motioned for us to gather at center ring. We walked toward him. "Look 'em inna eyes," Joe West said, leaning forward and whispering in my ear.

I did and a chill ran down my back. His eyes were dark and frightening. Deep-running rivers filled with sleepless nights and dreams. Reflections of what I once wanted to be.

But the fact that they were elemental was my hope. His style was set. He was a prisoner of age. I was sure he couldn't change for he was almost thirty. I was the outsider, the rough, unfinished kid. I was twenty-three.

Carlos Monzon and I touched gloves and Joe West led me back to my corner.

"Shake my hand," Joe West said, nodding to me. "An' take care a business." His voice was full of confidence. I grasped his hand and didn't want to let go. But he winked at me and then bent through the ropes. I turned to face Monzon. Beads of sweat broke out on my forehead. He just waited patiently for the bell.

2

High School, Seattle 1966

GYM CLASS WAS OVER. As I stood in the shower and let the hot water roll over my body, I felt good. In high school it wasn't difficult to feel that way. A mere shower after a particularly vigorous workout could cleanse and refresh every thought.

What I would do now was what I did almost every day. I would dress, drive home to my parents' suburban Seattle home on Lake Washington, and either mow the rich, green acre of lawn or weed the expensively shrubbed garden. My father, an engineer and geologist, had worked a lifetime to produce this house and my mother, who managed the local Sears-Roebuck, had helped him.

After the chores were over, I would usually make some phone calls to various girl friends for a Friday night date or some afternoon sortie. Too many cars, too many rooms with television sets, and too many meaningless things to do. The "light" at the end of the tunnel was college, something I was not at all sure I wanted. As a high school football hero with fairly good grades, the whole thing would be too easy. Just going on to college did not suit my personal idea of style. I enjoyed being the daredevil, the guy with enough guts to do something differently than everybody else.

I turned off my shower and picked up a towel, wrapping it around me as I walked back to my locker, past empty shoes and hanging clothes. I stepped gingerly on the polished concrete so I wouldn't slip.

"Hey," said my friend Robb, entering the dressing room. "You showing up for the fight today?"

"For what?" I said opening my locker.

"The fight," he said importantly. "The fight you agreed to last week." Everyone in the room heard the word "fight" and quickly gathered around us.

"When did I agree to that?" I asked nonchalantly.

"You know what I'm talking about." All eyes focused on me.

"I do?"

He nodded smugly. "You were at the party, and so were most of these guys. They heard you agree to it." Heads nodded. Robb had lots of supporters.

I forced a nervous grin to my lips. "Well, how serious can you be at a party?"

"What's wrong?" Robb said sarcastically. "Big Golden Gloves fighter afraid of a real fight?" That made everyone laugh. I had fought in the GG, albeit not that successfully to this point.

"Afraid?" I replied. "What have I got to be scared of?"

"This guy drinks a six-pack every day," Robb answered, barely concealing his enjoyment. "He's one tough mother."

I felt cornered. "Okay, big deal. But only six rounds and with gloves."

"He's already agreed to that."

"Oh," I said. "And with a referee, too."

"You got it."

"And judges," I said, hedging my bit even further.

I closed my locker and faced them. "Okay," I said. "I'll be there at four o'clock then."

That brought everyone to a fever pitch, and they all dashed for their lockers to get dressed. "Boy, it's about time we saw him really fight," someone said under his breath, trying not to let me hear it.

"Yeah," came the answer. "This guy he's fighting is rough. Beat the shit out of somebody up at the root beer stand last week."

I buttoned my shirt slowly, listening. That's typical, I thought, to be trapped by my own bold pronouncements. But they had a right to see what they had been hearing about for so long.

It started when I began promoting the grudge fights as a senior in high school on my neighbor's tennis court. I would draw up the posters for the fight, charge a quarter admission, and as the resident "expert" referee them. The posters always had me written in for the main event with a champion from another school. But those other school champions never showed up either, allowing me to lay claim to their territory. I owned the east side of town without ever fighting. They had never shown up because I had made them up. I was like most good promoters. Need an attraction? Make him up.

Everyone called me "Kat" then, referring to my quickness on the football field and as a Golden Gloves boxer. A few of them even formed a Kat membership club. They printed up a few cards at the shop at school and sold them for a quarter. With the card, you could get in the Kat-promoted fights for nothing.

I was quite a promoter back in those days. For another quarter, anyone around school could punch my stomach. It was often painful, but a quarter soon turned into a dollar, which turned into a six-pack of beer for Friday night parties. It was at one of those parties that the people around school had gotten together and found their own contender to challenge me for the east side championship.

There was no way they were going to get me to admit I was scared. So after school that day I had a friend drive me to Denny Park. It was several acres of grass and trees and streams. Quaint bridges were everywhere. And Lake Washington formed the park's entire western shore. It was too beautiful a place to have a fight, I thought. Especially one against some six-pack drinking legend whose prowess had grown each time one of his friends described him.

When we arrived the place was full of cars. Dozens of people had showed up. "Shit," my friend Dave said as he found a spot to park. "Did you think it would be this big?"

"I knew it," I said biting my lip.

Dave, who was serving as my manager, and I made our way through the throng to where everyone had gathered. A ring had been created by pulling four picnic tables together at right angles. It was a large ring and people surrounded us, hanging onto and spilling off of the benches and tabletops.

I tried to strut as I walked to the center of the ring. "Okay, let's get this going." An Ace bandage on each hand served as my handwraps. I also wore red satin trunks and tennis shoes. Everyone gawked at my outfit.

"Give him the gloves, Dave," I said pointing toward my opponent. He walked across the ring and held out four odd-shaped, mismatched gloves. They chose two and Dave gave me what remained.

"Did you see him?" I asked Dave as I pulled on the gloves.

Dave nodded and told me he looked tough. I glanced over and then saw him. He did look tough. He was stripped to the waist, wearing faded blue jeans, with bare feet. His hair was dark, topping off an angular face. He was the type of kid who would be the first to shave in the class.

"He's supposed to have been drinking all day," Dave said. "See if you can tire him out."

I checked his eyes. They did seem a little red. My strategy was formed instantly. "Just make sure it's six rounds."

You could tell who the people were for by where they sat. My good friends were directly in my corner. Kids in my gym class off to either side. Those I knew slightly were even farther removed. On the other side, I saw no friends at all.

A cowbell rang, splitting the afternoon air with an odd clank. I wasn't quite sure who or what I was facing here so I attempted to stay away from him at first. I kept moving, hoping to get him tired. He didn't appear to see it that way. He attacked me viciously, putting his reputation on the line with each swing. When he hit me it hurt.

I kept moving, trying to duck countless lefts and rights. His people were screaming, mine were silent, though some cheerleaders from my school were chanting my name in unison. In a clinch I looked at them, and thought about how odd they looked in their school-color uniforms. I pushed out of the clinch, feeling threatened for the first time. My reputation was just as much on the line as his.

Then he rushed in again. I ducked a wild swing and countered hard with my right. He went down to one knee. The referee ruled it a knockdown. Though I thought it was a slip, I didn't argue. That knockdown would give me the round. As he got to his feet the bell rung.

"Good round," Dave said, giving me a sip of Coke. "Press him a little more. He's getting tired."

The bell rang for the second round, and he attacked me again. If he was getting tired, he was concealing it well. I took the offensive. I jabbed, and threw a hard right hand. I knocked him on his ass. The momentum of the right hand kept me moving in, and I had my left hand cocked, ready to fire off a left hook. But he sat on the grass, just looking dazed. Instinct grabbed hold and made me throw it. It smashed into his head as he sat there while the crowd screamed "foul." I shrugged, knowing what it was. The bell came again, ending the second round.

"What'd you hit him when he was down for?" Dave berated me during my minute's rest.

"Because he was open," I said.

"You lost that round by disqualification. It was your round, too," he added disgustedly.

The bell started the third. This time he came at me more carefully. He was a little taller than me, and had a longer reach. That meant he could just stay away from me if he wanted. All he would have to do is hold his hand out and push it into my face.

He kept punching and took the third round. I won the fourth with more crisp punching, but I was beginning to feel a little tired myself. Then strange things began happening. The referee walked toward us and waved his hands. "Fight's over," he said.

"What?" Dave screamed. "It's supposed to be a six-rounder."

"More, more," the crowd yelled.

Then the referee, a kid a year older than me who didn't want to see either of us disabled, announced his decision. A draw.

"A draw?" my side shouted, wanting to see a fight to the finish.

"A draw?" his manager queried.

"A draw?" Dave echoed.

"A draw?" I hollered, firmly relieved that the whole thing was over.

Then the referee quieted down the crowd and looked at me. "Yeah, it's a draw. I took the second round away from you because you fouled. You hit him when he was down." He looked at me as if waiting for a complaint. Then he turned to my opponent. "So you each get two rounds then, a draw."

"What do you think?" Dave asked me as the crowd hollered and begged for more. I told him that I thought it foolish to argue, but that I thought I won it anyway. I was angry. I didn't feel I should lose the fight on a foul.

"Besides," I said to Dave as I pointed to my opponent, "he looks too tired to go any more."

But the crowd kept demanding for more, so irresolutely that my opponent and I squared off again. But just as we did, a gruff, grave voice came from the back of the crowd.

"Go on! Get outta here. This is a public park and you can't gather like this. It's against the law." It was the park director who lived across the street. "Who got hurt here, anyway," he added, looking around. Seeing no one hurt, he shooed us all off, still grumbling about our illegal activities.

"You looked good," Dave said to me, as he leaned against the car and fondled the gloves. I took my handwraps off and tried to look serious.

"Yeah," the referee nodded, joining us. "You had it won all the way. Except for the foul."

"No help from you," I said curtly.

"Aw, everyone could tell who the real fighter was," he replied.

Dave agreed quickly. "You can be champ some day, man. I know it."

"You really think so?" I asked, rubbing a swelling cheek.

3

Joe West

"Is THAT HIM?" Dave whispered. "You sure we want to do this?" he added.

"Yup. Come on," I said. "I want to meet Joe West."

We approached the tall man cautiously. He puffed intently on a cigarette and gazed into Yesler Street in the heart of Seattle's black section. It was empty, save for a few cars that passed by. The light from the cigarette lit his face.

"Who are you?" he said as I drew up to him. His eyes ran up and down my body. Dave stood behind me and held his breath.

"A fighter," I said.

"No kiddin'," he said squinting and forming a small smile on his face. "An' who's that?" he asked pointing at Dave.

"My manager."

"What does he manage?"

"Me!" I said in surprise.

His eyes traveled over both of us then and he nodded to himself. "What a yah doin' here then? I got fight business t'take care of." When he said the word "fight" he puffed up with importance.

"I want to fight for the team you're putting together."

"You wanna fight, huh?" he said. I nodded and he stared at me.

Behind him in the building were three black fighters moving around an old ring with garden hoses for ropes. Dave spied them and said, "Let us fight one of them."

Us? I thought, looking back at Dave.

"Yah wanna fight one a them?" Joe West asked, as if one of them would probably kill me.

I shrugged, "Yeah," as I jabbed Dave in the ribs for getting me into this.

Joe West seemed to be enjoying himself and walked into the building. Dave and I waited outside. He wheeled around and stared at us. "Well, yah can't fight 'em from out there."

Joe West was part Indian and part Negro. He liked telling people it was Joe, as in Joe Louis, and West, as in John Wayne. "That's where I get my Injun part, too," he'd chuckle, "John Wayne."

Joe West had been around prizefighting all of his life. First in Seattle, then in Los Angeles, and finally back to Seattle again. His deeply lined face had fifty-odd years of battles in diverse West Coast arenas in it. His was a thin but handsome face, with small, pencil-thin, gray moustache below the nose. He was also stoop-shouldered, a hundred lost bouts seemed to weigh him down.

But Joe was not a somber man nor an unhappy one. He had a great laugh, a cackle really, accompanied by a hiss each time he found something funny. It was a hustler's laugh, an optimist's laugh, one that I wanted to get to know. Joe West lived with dreams and futures, travel and fights.

I had heard about Joe West from my first boxing teacher, a black, jut-jawed man by the name of Bearcat Baker. Dave and I were just entering high school when we answered his Yellow Pages' ad about the art of self-defense, and when we first saw him on the top floor of Seattle's only fight gym, we knew he was the man to teach us how to fight.

Bearcat walked proudly around the gymnasium, with his thickly muscled arms protruding from a worn T-shirt that topped off baggy dungarees held up by black suspenders. And when he talked to you he talked politely through his gold teeth. The others had been long ago separated from his mouth.

Bearcat taught us to box for thirty dollars a month, three days a week. He went slowly, working on one thing until we had it down, and then moving on.

Finally, Bearcat declared us ready and then got Dave and I amateur fights. Dave beat a guy by the name of Joe Moses (the toughest son of a bitch alive, he told me afterward) and I fought a Jim Stone, knocking him out in one round (proving that names don't really mean much). For that first fight I called myself Willie Pastrano III. I remember one wag at ringside saying, "A red-headed wop? I don't believe it!"

But I got a trophy for my efforts and ran home to show it to everyone. I told them that I wanted to be a prizefighter. They thought it was cute. They knew that every suburban, middle-class kid at one time either wanted to join the Foreign Legion, fight Indians, or climb Mt. Everest. They knew I'd one day become a bank executive or insurance salesman. Everything in the suburbs is like that. All planned out.

Bearcat then entered me in the Golden Gloves. Dave by this time had quit to become my manager. I lost my first fight in the Golden Gloves. Dave then told Bearcat to enter me in the next tournament. He did and I lost to the same man. Bearcat soberly appraised my two losses and told me there was nothing more he could teach me. He sent me to Joe West, the man to talk to about becoming a real fighter.

I played high school football for a year with that thought on my mind. When I heard Joe West was forming his own Golden Gloves team, I decided to visit him.

That first day I remember working the black fighters over pretty good. Seeing that I was a white kid who could fight made them take me into their confidence. They talked of things that were alien to my experience—jail, drugs, and whores. Two of the fighters were part-time pimps who would often have their women come into the gym and watch them work out. That upset Joe West, but he found it in his nature to let people be themselves, for better or worse.

Joe West disliked my newly acquired speech patterns. I began shortening my sentences and talking tough like the other team members. He drew me aside one day and waved a finger in my face. "Don't be talkin' that jive shit, man." He said, "Good talk'll get it before that. Education aw'ways beats ignorance."

I listened to him and dropped my tough-guy act.

Joe West spent the next months showing me the tricks of the trade; how to roll with punches, counter, foul, and win. He had a vast knowledge of the game.

After a couple more losing Golden Gloves efforts, he took me aside. "You'll never be a good amateur," he said. "Yah wait back like a pro. Yah wait for the other guy t'make a mistake. But in a six-minute fight there ain't no time t'wait."

All I wanted to do was fight professionally. Still a cute idea, thought my parents. Like the rest of my tribe, I was bundled up and sent to college. That same year I won the Northwest GG championships, surprising everyone but Joe West.

"It was tactics, man. We gotta outsmart 'em," he winked.

"Tactics?"

"Yeah, yah win fights by thinkin' with yer head. We can work together an' win. Yah do it like yah was hustlin' cards. Yah never let 'em know yer outthinkin' 'em."

I agreed and wanted to go pro again. Joe West said no, that he had to let me try for the Olympics that were coming up in 1968, and stay in college. I tried, won the Northwest crown again, and then lost in the national championships. Joe and I both knew it was a wasted effort. All we ever talked about was tactics and professional fighting.

When I wasn't fighting, I was playing college football, and Joe West had something against that. "Don't be fuckin' with the big guys," he'd say. I told him I was just staying in shape.

I didn't like team sports now that I had had a taste of prizefighting. Team sports have a tendency to mold a player into something less than he really is. No team endeavor could conjure up the spectacle of violence and pain that one man facing another half-naked in the canvas ring could. Only there did I receive the rare and vivid glimpses of authentic spirit that inhabited a prizefighter's soul.

"Let's go pro," I said to Joe after my losing effort at the 1968 national championships.

He winked and said, "Yep, yer ready for it now."

I returned home after my second year of college was over and told my parents what my plans were. I told them that I was going to be moving to Los Angeles with Joe West so I could become a prizefighter. They were shocked.

"Why there?" they both asked.

"Joe West said it was learn to fight down there, or die!" I said dramatically. The truth was that Joe West had a hard time getting a young fighter the proper action in Seattle. To learn to fight is to stay busy, and in Seattle there was a fight card only every four months or so. Joe West told me that in California a man could fight once a week if he wanted.

"But why a boxer?" my mom and dad still asked, their dreams of college for me and the good life seemingly evaporating. I think they must have wondered where they had failed.

I looked at my dad, a crusty, former diamond miner–turned engineer, and shrugged. "I just know I can do it, Dad."

I merely wanted to do something different. And I knew

that they would eventually support my decision, figuring it to be nothing but a whim anyway.

"Well," my dad said, looking at my mom for support, "you have to be careful then, if this is what you want to do. Boxing can take all you have and never give it back."

I thought he had seen one too many fight movies.

4

On The Road

A MONTH LATER, the first week in June 1968, Joe West and I were on the road for Los Angeles. As Joe made the sweeping, gradual turn to enter the freeway, he sighed, settling back into the seat for a hard day's driving.

"Yep, this is on the road for real," he said, pausing for a moment to let his words sink in.

My eyes took in the Seattle skyline and the jutting mountains that silhouetted it. They stood together, powerful and calm, steel and concrete surrounded by forest.

Joe West watched the speedometer and coaxed the old station wagon ahead. When it reached sixty miles per hour he leveled off. "Think yer ready for it?" he asked, glancing at me.

"I better be . . ." I said.

"Yep, jus' like the old days," Joe West said, leaving his eyes on the road. "Takin' on all comers an' fightin' 'em in their hometowns. It's jus' like my pop and me runnin' these roads again. I'll tell yah, we colored folks had t'be hustlers for real. Whiskey, women, gas stamps . . . you name 'em. We had t'do it."

"When was that?" I asked.

He smiled again. "Back inna thirties an' forties. My ma weaned me onna road here. We'd jus' sit inna back there an' watch that man drive."

Joe West then chuckled to himself. His smile made the memories more pleasant.

Joe cleared his throat, one of his signals that he wanted to talk business. "Yer folks sure tried t'hang on t'the end, didn't they?"

"Yeah, they did." My mother had locked herself in the bathroom, refusing to see me leave. She was scared. My father was resolute but not too happy about the whole state of affairs.

"Didn't they like the contract?" Joe West asked.

I opened my palms and tilted my head. "They just didn't like the option clause that tied me to one man for six years." Then I laughed. "What would you do if your son wanted to be a prizefighter?"

"I wouldn't let 'im," Joe West said. "But yer dad didn't have t'wait till the last minute t'get the thing notarized. We'd been after 'im for a week t'get it done. He knew I needed it to be your guardian. Yer just still a twenty-year-old kid."

I agreed and remembered again. Dad didn't like the contract. It was a standard one for three years, but also with a clause that gave Joe West another three-year option on my services. Everyone at home had hoped I'd change my mind.

"Well, if we can't do it in three years . . ." I said.

"Oh, man," Joe West said. "There's people inna fight game that been around for ten years, and still tryin' t'make it. Three years might be pushin' it."

"I think we can get there," I said. "But what my dad really didn't like was the way the money was split. He thought you should get just what the contract specified, instead of a flat 50 percent. He thought I should get the specified two-thirds and you one-third."

"Yeah but I'm payin' all expenses outta my half. We're gonna be onna road for a long time. If yah want t'pay yer own expenses, then . . ."

"No, no," I said. "I'm happy with it. They just thought it might be the usual semantical treachery from a manager, that's all."

"Aw'right, this is the way I see it. Yer not givin' anythin' up for the 50 percent yah give me, but I'm givin' yah a solid 50 percent outta my connections and experience. Yah can't get no fights unless yah know someone." Then Joe West paused again and smiled. "Now what's semantical treachery?"

"That's where the dimwitted fighter gets lied to," I answered, grinning.

"I don't lie t'no one," Joe West said forthrightly.

"Me neither," I said.

Joe West smiled. "That's one aw'ready."

"What?"

"A lie," he said glancing at me. "Yah never told me about those Seattle businessmen that wanted t'buy yer contract. Why not?"

Joe had me. My faced flushed red. "I didn't like their deal, that's why."

"What'd they say?"

"Awww, it was no big deal." I wanted to change the subject.

"Look, yah gotta start tellin' me everythin'. That's the only way we can make it. Yer smart enough t'make yer own decisions about fightin' people. But if yah don't tell me everythin', then I can't protect yah."

"From what?"

"Fight riffraff," Joe West answered. "Now what kinda deal did these guys offer?"

"A lot of money," I said. "They were going to keep me in Seattle, and get me a good teacher."

"That all?"

"Well, no. They talked about big television fights and things."

"And things?"

"Well, guaranteed advancement and stuff, whatever that is," I snickered.

Joe West nodded slowly, understanding something I didn't. Then he gave me a sideways look. "And what'd they say about me?"

I pretended to ignore the question, but when he asked again I looked at him and watched his reaction. "They called you a nigger son of a bitch, and a butcher. They said you would take me out of town and get me hurt. They said you had to take me out of town because they wouldn't let niggers promote fighters here. That's where they blew it."

"Where? Calling me a nigger? I been called that before."

"No, saying they were going to keep me in town. I wanted to hit the road. Besides, listening to what they say, and to what you say, made up my mind to go with you. You were the only one who said I couldn't fight good enough yet to live. They tried to feed my ego."

"Yer right there," he then said. "The road is the only thing that'll teach yah t'fight for yer life. That's what it gives yah," he said pointing down it again. "That knack'a survival. That's what yah gotta develop. And these lessons aren't easily forgotten either, not like the school ones yah forget the minute after."

"I don't know. College was okay for awhile, but it didn't push me. I just grew tired of it. But I might go back."

"It's a lot easier 'n prizefightin', that's for sure."

"That was it," I said, watching Joe West reach down for a cup of coffee out of the plaid thermos he kept at his side. "I didn't want anything that easy."

Joe West chuckled. "You'll get that in prizefightin' aw'right. And like I said, yah won't forget the things it'll teach yah."

He gave me another quick glance and sipped his coffee, bearing down on the wheel as the scenery flashed by.

Joe West was an intense driver. There was no one better to get you from point A to point B. He had developed the necessary stamina early on. First, jousting with his father and then later with a string of prizefighters.

"I wanna get t'the middle of California tonight," Joe West stated, still sipping his coffee.

He drove hard through southern Washington and Oregon, over flat roads and mountain passes, past homes and people who stood in their gardens and watched us glide by. Seeing the gear-laden station wagon, they would wave and smile. It felt good to be going somewhere. I imagined they were envious of us and our freedom.

"Here comes California," Joe said, as we crossed the state line. He slowed the car and pulled behind a line of cars being checked for fruit and other foods that might be carrying dangerous insects into the state. A tall, uniformed man then walked up to Joe's window and told us to pull over to the side to be checked more closely. The other cars were quickly allowed to pass. After they checked and didn't find anything, they motioned us through.

"That's what yah get with travelin' with a nigger son of a bitch," Joe West said loudly, watching the tall man grow smaller in the rear-view mirror. "Happens every time. And they ain't found nothin' yet."

The statement was funny at first hearing, but it grew oppressive and filled the car for the next hour, stifling conversation. And as we drove through the dusty plain of the San Joaquin Valley, Joe silently watched tired, brown-faced farm workers laboring. At least he was moving. They were not.

"Yah know," Joe West said, snapping out of his trance. "Yer the first white prizefighter I had down here. That's good luck."

"Why?" I asked.

He smiled slightly and said, "There's a God that looks out for white prizefighters, man."

Again, I was shocked almost speechless. "Yeah," I agreed hollowly.

"Yep, I'll tell yah. I had better fighters 'n you down here, but they was all black, confused. They wanted the same things yah do, but they didn't wanna work t'get 'em. They thought it would be given to 'em." Then Joe laughed. "Ain't nothin' given to no black prizefighter. Nothin'."

I didn't want to say that I was also a little confused, so I agreed again. Nor did I ask him about the inflection in his voice that inferred I was different because I was white.

When I thought about that, I guess Joe did treat me differently. He was easier on me than he was with the black fighters I had seen him with. He had to push them to be better than they thought they could be, whereas I picked up things right off the bat. He knew that for a black fighter, the ring would be the only thing that man could do so he'd better get good at it. With me, he knew I could give it up anytime for something else. And I didn't bother to argue about his explanation on why they didn't make it, or that his whole explanation seemed too patented and easy for such a complication. Joe West just kept driving and smiling.

We stopped that first day at a bizarre combination of bus stop and paper-shack motel. The owner met our arrival. He was small and roundish, and he sweated a lot. His eyes asked too many questions as he regarded this thin black man and small white kid. He started to form a question on his lips, directed at me.

"Prizefighter," Joe West then said, arching a thumb in my direction. "I'm his manager."

The man nodded, but didn't believe him. His eyes darted back to me and I nodded.

Joe West remarked the guy had quite a setup here. The man answered, mumbled his thanks, and led Joe and me to our room. The room became dimly lit when Joe West hit the switch. There was one small bed, which sagged in the middle, and one full-sized cot. Joe West fell on the cot and pulled a tuna fish sandwich out of a brown paper bag.

"Here, it'll give yah some meat. A prizefighter gotta have meat to fight."

I took the sandwich and munched. Joe checked his watch and looked at me. "Better get some sleep, man, after you finish that. Mornin' comes early for prizefighters."

I slid into bed and watched him reach for the light switch. A cockroach bolted onto the floor, scurrying erratically, wondering perhaps about the intrusion. I slept soundly.

5

Society Red

Morning did come early and with a bang. Joe and I were just stirring in our beds when a kicking and crashing sound came from outside the door. I lifted my head and saw him reach inside one of his shoes and remove his penknife, generally called "the protector" and familiarly known as Henry. He leaped to the door and stood, knife blade gleaming in the darkness.

"Who's there . . ." he said. There was another kick and a thump.

"Six o'clock," said the man who had given us the room.

Joe West glanced at me and shook his head. "That son of a . . . ," and he pulled open the door. "Yah said what?"

I don't know if the man saw the blade, but he meekly said it was time to get up.

Joe West growled. "Go easy onna door or I'll sic my prizefighter on yah." The man leaned to one side, saw me sitting in bed, and nodded.

"Prizefighter, huh?"

Joe West shut the door. "Damn bet'cha." Then he snapped his wrist and folded the knife into its handle.

As Joe West drove hard again, he still talked tactics and

the road, and about the men in Seattle who had tried to steal me from him. I didn't want to talk about it but it seemed to bother him.

"What were they gonna give yah?" he asked.

"Guaranteed advancement and stuff," I said again. "But that's what I didn't want, Joe. I wanted to hit the road."

"Be a freewheeler, huh?" Joe West said, glancing at me.

"The road will guarantee me something," I replied. "I'll learn to fight on it."

Joe West shook his head tiredly. "Road ain't shit, man. Ain't shit to be runnin' up an' down it all yer life. Ain't no guarantees from this here road." He pointed toward it and let his arm fall again.

"Well," I said. "We can make our name on it, and then go home for some big fights."

"Ain't that easy," Joe West replied. "With the guys inna Seattle fight game now, yah jus' about have t'go with the okey-doke."

"Okey-doke?"

He nodded. "Yeah, that what they called guaranteed advancement. Fight riffraff. I don't unnerstand it. They got four promoters in town, all cuttin' each other's throat! That's why yah gotta talk to me. I can protect yah from that shit."

"I'll talk," I said.

"What kinda money were they talkin' about?" Joe West then asked.

"Good money, good promo," I said. "But shoot, their money wasn't important. It never has been."

"Yah know middleweights don't make that much," Joe West nodded.

"I know."

"You'll probably get seventy-five bucks for yer first one," he said. "An' halfa that is mine."

"You're entitled to it," I said.

Joe West bore down on the wheel. A while later he cleared

his throat and asked, "Yah tell 'em I was takin' yah t'Los Angeles?"

I nodded. "That's when they called you the nigger butcher."

Joe West looked over and smiled, and then made a violent face, snarling up his teeth. "Maybe I am . . . Maybe I am."

We laughed together and talked tactics. The traffic began to thicken, tall buildings appeared on the horizon. "We're just about there," Joe West said.

"I can tell."

"Yep. The action's fast around here."

I threw a few punches into the air and ducked a bug that splattered against the windshield. Joe West watched me and chuckled to himself. "Yah shoulda countered 'em. Yah aw'-ways wanna counter after yah duck. Keeps the guy off yah."

"But this was a bug," I grinned.

"What say we drive on down t'the Strip. Look at the hippies an' things."

"Okay," I said, and away we went.

Joe drove slowly on the Strip, telling stories about each place. He'd point out girls and whistle at them. Then, as we passed a place with a catchy name, he'd say, "Yah gotta have a identifiable name. That way, people'll remember just who yah are. Yah fight down here a couple a times the promoter'll probably give yah one. He called one a my fighters Frenchy once."

"I don't want a name like that," I said thinking it over. "I already have one, remember? When we first got together you gave me one. I wrote a poem about it, used to perform it in front of my high school class."

"Yeah? What name's that?"

"Society Red. Remember?"

Joe West frowned. "Let's hear that poem."

I grinned and slapped the dashboard in time to the meter of the poem. "My name is Red from society/ I come to fight and to riot-ey/ I don't play with women with hair that's long,/

I'm Society Red and I can't go wrong/ For I'm Society, Society Red/ It's way past four before I go to bed."

Joe West burst into a cackle and collapsed against the steering wheel. "You did that in fronta people?"

"Yeah, there's more," I said, knowing that I had him going. "I'm called Society because it fits my clothes/ I'm always looking good and everyone knows/ That when Society Red comes to town,/ There's going to be some heads beaten into the ground/ Because I'm Society and I have to be cool/ For it's them fighters I'm going to rule."

Joe West kept a grin on his face and bounced around in the seat as I sang the poem. "His name is Red from society . . ." he said, then turned to me and nodded, "That's what yah are then: Society Red."

"You like it?" I laughed.

Joe West pulled in front of a large hotel. It was pink and seemed to typify Southern California. "We aren't staying here?" I said, thinking that a pink hotel wasn't exactly the way a prizefighter should start a career.

Joe West nodded and motioned for me to get my bag. He grabbed his and lurched out of the seat. The poem was on his lips and he still chuckled to himself.

"We'll be here just a day or two," Joe West answered. He registered me and rode the elevator to the upper floors of the hotel. After checking behind all of the doors, he pronounced it all right.

"Here," Joe West then said, reaching into his pocket and pulling money out. "Take this an' get somethin' t'eat. I gotta go find a place t'put yah."

I took the bill and concealed it from him. "What makes you think I can get something with a dollar?"

He was just wheeling around to the door and stopped. "That was a five, man."

"How can you tell?" I scoffed. "You just reached in and pulled one out."

Joe West smiled and put his finger in the air. "It's the process of elimination, the same game yer in. Yah see the ones is aw'ways ripped and frayed around the edges. The fives less so, and on up. Yah just feel the edges."

"Why not just pull it out? And look at it?"

He squinted and drew his head back. "Man, the first thing yah learn onna streets is t'keep what yah got in yer pocket a secret. Yah wanna have secrets onna street."

With that said Joe West turned quickly and left the room. I listened to his footsteps in the hall and the elevator doors, and then he was gone. I looked at the bill. It was a five.

I decided to take a walk after awhile. Joe West had told me I'd be getting my professional start soon, and I knew where it was going to happen. The Olympic Auditorium, at Eighteenth Avenue and Grand Street, just down the road from the hotel.

I hit the street looking for it. Finally I spied it. It was a large, rectangular, concrete building, and surrounded by freeways, parking lots, and warehouses on the other sides.

I walked to it boldly. It was the kind of building I didn't have to sneak up on. It's very appearance seemed to be a partial reward for sweat and sacrifice. As I closed in on it I heard every scream and foot-stomping boo that had ever been expressed there. Such sounds never leave buildings like that; they remain to give it clattering life.

The Olympic Auditorium was a tarnished symbol from the golden age of boxing. Started in the Joe Louis era by Eileen and Cal Eaton, it's seen better days. But with help from people like matchmakers Mickey Davies and Don Chargin, a pair of straight shooters, the place underwent a renaissance in the mid-sixties. They brought a badly needed respect back to boxing. Parents who had been buying nothing but footballs and baseballs for their children again started giving them boxing gloves.

The Olympic promotions were prizefighting's best and

should have been an example for the rest of boxing. The promoters didn't take the money and run, but reinvested it. They developed a pension fund of sorts for retired prizefighters. And they knew when to deny a fighter a license to fight. Where in most other states a blind man could get a license to fight, at the Olympic, a medical exam took all day.

Standing outside the building I wanted to become part of it. All I knew now was that its long and narrow corridors were littered with past champions' and challengers' pictures. I wondered which I would be.

Then I laughed at myself for being such a dreamer and walked back to the hotel. Again my thoughts drifted to toughening myself up for what promised to be a long grind ahead. As I slid into bed I wondered where Joe was. Then I smiled, happy again to be a dreamer. Joe West had told me only the dreamers made it big in prizefighting.

As I turned out the light, I tried to remember Joe West ever talking about the present. He never did, like maybe he didn't believe in it. It was always the future. "If a guy ain't got dreams," he would say, "he be stuck inna past. Shit, man, the past ain't gonna pay the rent."

6

The Gym

"C'MON, SOCIETY, let's get it on," I heard Joe West say through the door the next morning. "I got a place for yah t'stay." He sounded excited and happy.

"Great," I mumbled, rolling out of bed. "Where is it?" I asked opening the door.

"Ten or fifteen minutes from here," he said bursting past me rubbing his hands. "Society, I'll tell yah. We're just plain lucky t'get set so quick."

I grabbed my bag and followed him to the car. We drove for a few minutes through pastel-shaded suburbs.

"Man we're lucky," Joe West said again. He twisted his head once quickly. "I gotta know yer in a safe place."

I nodded and watched him turn onto a street where the homes were all small and white, with neatly manicured lawns. Palm trees pushed against the sky. "What kind of a place is this?" I asked, getting caught up in his excitement.

"A good place," he said.

"Oh, you know the people?"

He shook his head. "No, but a friend a mine does."

I thought for a moment. "Are they black or white?"

He paused, and gave me a sideways look. "Black, like me."

I nodded again, watching Joe West check out the addresses and slow down. Our tires scraped against the curb. "Here 'tis," Joe West said.

He jumped out of the car and urged me to follow. We walked over a lawn, past a box-shaped house to the back. He gave a penetrating look to the back porch. "There it is," he said.

"Where?" I asked.

"C'mon," he said walking up a few steps, and inserting a key, pushing open a door. "How do yah like it?"

I followed him and looked around. It was an empty room, save for a small bed and table with a lamp on it. "Give me a minute," I said, walking in. I checked out the bathroom, saw a large tub, and nodded. "It looks okay."

"For forty bucks a month it's a palace," Joe said eagerly. "Now that we're set, we can get t'the gym this afternoon, get goin'."

I nodded, and looking at the one bed said, "Guess we'll have to get another bed."

"What?" Joe West said.

"Another bed."

He shook his head. "Can't. It's too small a place for two. I'll be stayin' with some friends just a little ways from here. Besides, the worst thing fer us is t'get tired to seein' each other. A fighter gotta be by hisself, get that knacka survivin'."

Joe took me to the gym that afternoon. He gave me a choice of a couple of places to train. One was downtown Los Angeles, and one was in Watts. I said Watts because I thought it sounded better for a fighter to say he trained in Watts.

Joe West agreed but tempered it by saying he didn't want to make that our camp. "Don't like all that riotin' action," he said.

But today it was Watts. Joe West drove to what looked like an old, broken-down garage and parked the car. Shiny, new cars sat outside of it and small black children played carelessly in the street.

"These are fighters' cars," Joe West said as we made our way through and around them. "Yah can always tell. The good ones have good cars."

Standing at the doorway to the gym was an old man, short and crusty-looking but with a gleam in his eyes. He grinned at Joe West and they shook hands. It was Jake Shugrue.

Jake looked like his name. His face was a reservoir of lines and years. He looked bloated and older than his sixty-odd years. But he was also a legend in Los Angeles fight circles. It was because he knew fighters. They said that Jake Shugrue could look at a kid and tell whether he'd be any good or not. If that was true, the knowledge came from his eyes; small slits in the middle of skin waves.

Joe West talked with Jake about the old times for a while, and gave me a chance to look around. The gym had two large rings in it that took up most of the space. Two large punching bags stood off to the side, next to where aging fighters watched themselves in long rectangular mirrors.

Jake Shugrue's gym attracted a hungry mob that surrounded the rings as men sparred with each other. As each duo tangled, the bets began to flow. Sides were chosen and the winner would be remembered only until the next two fighters climbed into the ring.

Jake helped Joe and I. As I was to spar that day, everyone wanted to test the new kid. Jake would stand over and watch as Joe West would shoot a glance at him, and either nod yes or no to whoever asked us. Joe West didn't want anybody testing me too much, apparently.

But I did work, and well, and then I was no longer the new kid, but one of dozens of others trying to make a name for himself. Then Joe West called me over.

"Two weeks," he said simply. "Yah might be goin' in two. On the twenty-seventh."

I didn't smile at all. I just knew it was time to get to work. A prizefighter dies a little each time he's told there's going to be a fight.

"You'll be enterin' lonely territory," Joe West said. "An' yah better get used t'it."

7

The Olympic

JULY 27, 1968

I WAS RESTLESS. I stood up and paced across the simple room that Joe West had chosen for me. "Let's go, huh?" I said.

He raised his eyes over the top of the magazine to mine. "How yah feelin'?"

I gestured helplessly. Then I began pacing again and tightening my fists. It was the evening of my first fight.

"A little nervous, huh?" Joe West said, understanding my anxiety. "Well, we don't have t'be there for another hour yet."

I stopped in my tracks and faced him. "I know, but this waiting here is killing me. Can't we wait down there?" I tried not to whine. "Nothing could be worse than waiting here," I added.

Joe West began dragging himself to his feet. "Waiting down there is," he said. "But okay, if that's what yah want . . ."

"I can get ready down there better anyway," I stated, becoming happy that I was getting my wish. On the day of the fight, a prizefighter dare not let one wish go unanswered. He has to get in the habit of everything going his way.

We gathered the fight gear and moved outside to the car.

I listened to it sputter a few times, and then roar to life. I stepped in and we were off.

"Okay," Joe West said, entering traffic carefully. "Let's go over this again. I know yer tired of it, but yah should be. Yah always should get tired of the stuff that's important. That's how yah know it's important."

I turned in the seat and faced him. When he knew he had my attention, he began. "Aw'right," he said. "Now when the fight starts, yah listen t'me. Above all else yah listen t'me." He watched me and nodded to himself. "Now when I tell yah t'slice 'n' splice, what's that mean?"

"That there's only a minute left in the round," I said.

"And what?" Joe West asked.

"And time for a little action," I answered.

Joe West nodded. "Now it ain't gonna be easy t'hear me, what with the crowd and all. But yah gotta train yer ear too. I'm gonna be yer only friend in these things," he emphasized. "The Olympic Auditorium has a clock in it but I don't wanna see yah lookin' at it. I'm the one that'll tell yah where yah are."

"Slice and splice—minute left," I said.

Joe West lit a cigarette and puffed heavily on it. I gave him a discouraging look, and he noticed it. He snuffed it out. "Okay," he smiled. "Now what's 'take care a business' mean?"

"That there are only ten seconds left, and I should begin making my way to the corner so I can sit down quicker than the other guy," I said sighing, tired of going over and over this.

"Look," Joe said abruptly. "This stuff is important. If yer sittin' down and watchin' the other guy walk across the ring, that gives yah an extra eight seconds a rest. In a prizefight, that's like gold, brother."

"I know," I said defensively. "I'm listening."

"It takes more than listenin'," Joe West said. "When that

crowd gets t'hollerin', it'll be hard. Yah gotta get it in yer head natural, so yah know jus' how much is always required a yah in every round. That last-minute flurry yah do'll catch the judges' eyes. They only remember the last minute of a round anyway, and sittin' down as the bell rings'll give yah more rest."

"Well, make sure that stool is there when I sit," I said sarcastically. "I don't want to sit and end up on the floor. Now that would catch the judges' eyes."

Joe West laughed. "It's all tactics, man. Don't worry about nothin' but fightin' and listenin' t'me. Tactics'll win us fights."

"Slice and splice and take care of business," I said, as Joe West pulled into the Olympic Auditorium parking lot.

"You got it," he said, giving his head a half twist.

He locked up the car and we walked toward the fighters' entrance. Two security men made a motion to stop us. "I'm fighting tonight," I growled. "This is my manager."

They smiled tight grins and let us pass. "Yah like sayin' that, don't yah," Joe West said.

"Well, I am, right?"

When I didn't get an answer to that from Joe West, I glanced at him. His face was emotionless, and blank with neither a yes or no. I felt it was a challenge, that I had to prove I was a real prizefighter. I tightened my fist and mouth, knowing I had to win.

There was a large blackboard inside the building, with chalk names of all the fighters that were fighting. Joe West gave it a quick glance and led me down some steps through the catacombs of the auditorium to a dim corridor. Our footsteps echoed through them, and because we were so early, there was no one else around.

"You ever use this dressing room?" I asked, seeing Joe West pause in front of a numbered door and push it open.

"Once before, a year ago with a damn slow heavyweight,"

he said, grunting as he lifted the large canvas bag onto a table. I walked to a long bench and sat on it. Joe West rummaged around the bag and pulled out a towel. "Here," he said tossing it to me. "Wad it up and lay on yer back. Might as well get some rest. We sure got plenty a time."

The room was stark white and small. There was one bare bulb on the ceiling that a single fly buzzed around. A table and a bench, nothing else. A tough room for what I knew would be a tough night.

"Did the guy win?" I asked, raising my head off the bench.

"Did who win?" Joe West asked, busying himself with preparing the fight gear.

"The heavyweight, your other fighter."

"Yup," Joe West nodded. "Now, what's slice 'n' splice mean?"

I sighed and Joe West shot a quick glance to me. I knew I better not let him hear me do that again. I answered fast. "That there is a minute left, and I have to flurry to catch the judges' eyes."

He kept watching me and then nodded. "It'll help yah win fights," he said. "Not as much in these four rounders like tonight's, but in the tens. Yah gotta have tactics t'win fights. The best fighter is the one that's smart. An' that's where yah got it."

I lay my head back down on the towel on the bench. Gazing back to the light bulb, I saw the single fly joined by another. They alternated attacking the pipe in disguised patterns. "What's this guy's name again?" I asked, lifting my head up again.

Joe West grimaced and tried to ignore me. "Man, I been tellin' yah all I know about this guy all day. What'd yah wanna know now?"

"Just his name," I said.

"Johnson," Joe West answered. "Ronnie Johnson."

"Ron or Ronnie?"

"Ron."

"How many fights has he had?"

"Two . . . ," Joe West said, beginning to sound impatient.

"How many has he won?"

Joe West glanced at me, setting the handwraps aside, and looked into my eyes. "Will yah stop worryin'? The first punch'll be the hardest. After that, just stay in control."

I nodded and lay my head down again. But I was so full of questions I had to get answers. "How many?" I said.

"How many what?" Joe West said, in a low voice.

"Has he won?"

Joe started chuckling. "Okay, he's won one and drawn one. Two fights."

"Drawn one?" I said quickly, lifting my head again. "You said he lost one this afternoon." I panicked. Joe was fudging things. Unknowingly, he had taken away some of my confidence.

"Draw's as good as a loss," he said casually.

I still had my head lifted up, looking directly at him. "That's not what you said when I fought draws."

"Oh, man," Joe West said turning his head to me. "You never fought a draw in yer life."

"Well, what if I had?" I asked.

Joe West shrugged. "I'd hope yah learned from it, that's all."

It was a simple answer and satisfied me. I sighed and lay my head back down. Looking at the light bulb, I noticed the flies had left.

"What's that?" Joe West asked, hearing me sigh.

"Nothing," I said, and then seeing I had his attention, used it. "Is this guy black or white?"

"Black," Joe West said succinctly. Then he turned the question over in his head and straightened up from the table. "Now what fuckin' difference does that make?"

"It makes a difference," I said. "You should know everything about the guy you're fighting."

Joe West put his hands on his hips, and chuckled. "Yeah, yah might wanna borrow some money from 'em."

"No, I mean it," I said seriously. "Now that I know he's black, I'll fight him different."

"How then?"

"Work on his body more," I said. "Black fighters are always weak there. I don't think I can hurt him in the head."

Joe West looked puzzled for a second, and then slowly began to get my meaning. It was in that moment he knew I was still a white, middle-class kid. His eyes flashed a racial pride at me.

Casting aside my own ignorance, without a trace of a smile, he looked at me. "Okay. Yah work on this guy's body then. I want yah t'learn it anyway. Better start gettin' dressed now," he said, throwing me my gear. He had one ear trained on the noise of the people who were filling the arena. It promised to be a packed house tonight because two local favorites were fighting for the city championship.

I got to my feet and undressed from the bottom to the top. That was the way I always had done it when I was an amateur.

I pulled on my calf-high boxing shoes and tied them. Then I stepped into my large, tight-fitting leather cup that would protect me from wayward punches.

A former middleweight champ once told me that he won the championship by attacking a man's belt line, actually a foul. He said to hit a man in his liver and kidneys was to make him piss blood. That was something I sure didn't want to happen to me.

After the leather protector, I put my green velvet trunks over it. I slapped my midsection a few times and Joe West nodded. "Okay, let's get those hands."

He pulled a small, folding chair up that I sat in backward, straddling it, placing my hands on the backrest for support. This would be a new experience for me. In the professional ranks, a man can have as much tape as he wants on his hands. In the amateurs, you get no tape, just a specified amount of gauze.

"Aw'right, gimme yer left hand," Joe said. The left hand was always first. That was the one Joe West told me his friend Sonny Liston always started with. He then attacked my hands with gauze, winding long, two-inch strips around and around. Then hard tape would be added, around and around again. Then long strips of the hard tape would be placed between my fingers and stuck to the top of my hand at the wrist, and around to the palm of my hand to the wrist again. It all would be covered with more hard tape. When it was all finished my hands throbbed with an energy that I had never felt before.

"It's no accident people fight with their hands," Joe West said, inspecting his work. "Fortune teller'll tell yah; what yah got in yer head yah got in yer hands. That's how they read palms."

That made sense to me. Rising out of the seat, I threw a few punches. Joe put up his hands with his palms out. "Bang 'em," he said. I popped a few punches into them and he drew them back and winced. "Damn, yer punchin' harder 'n ever, Society."

I nodded again, and began to hunch my shoulders up and down. I felt grim. I started pacing again. Two steps this way, swing around, then two steps the other way. It was a small room and not made for pacers.

Joe West then took two aspirin out of a bottle and choked them down his throat. "Yah can have some after the fight," he said.

"I never take the stuff," I said.

"Aspirin?" Joe West asked, raising his eyebrows.

"Not any pills," I said. "Ever."

"That's good," Joe West said seriously, then cracking a smile. "I had a prizefighter once that took buckets of 'em before fights. That fool once drank a bottle of codeine cough syrup just as he was in the dressin' room loosenin' up."

"Hypochondriac," I said.

"No, there were no needles," Joe West said, mistaking my meaning. "Just pills."

I smiled. "What happened after he drank the medicine?"

"I didn't know he was doin' it," Joe West explained, starting to cackle. "Until I came back to the room from watchin' another fight, and this son of a bitch was sittin' and gigglin' on the floor."

"Make him fight?"

"Goddamn right," Joe West answered quickly. "He walked right into the best punches the other guy had."

I raised my own eyebrows. "Jesus, did he win the fight?"

"No, that same round after takin' all a the punches he woke up. The guy jabbed him once and he crumpled. Never saw such a fake," Joe West said, letting his voice trail off.

"What did you do then, with the guy on his back out there."

"I jumped in and asked him if he was aw'right. Well yah know what that son of a bitch did? He peeked at me and smiled."

"No . . ."

"Yep. I told that son of a bitch t'get up before I kicked him inna head," Joe West said, smiling all the time, yet serious. "Last time I saw him, too. Can't stand a quitter."

I listened to the story and actually forgot about my own fight. That was part of the Joe West method. He knew I was too tight. It was his job to get me loose. He always could pull a cornball story about a prizefighter out of his hat to relax me.

"Aw'right, let's get them eyes," Joe said, pulling a small bottle out of the fight bag.

"What are you going to do?" I asked apprehensively.

"Tilt yer head back. I'm gonna put this on."

"Let me see it," I said reaching out and taking the bottle. It was something called Newskin, and it was for covering cuts. It smelled like nail polish.

"It'll hold yer eyebrows together," he said. "Just tilt yer head back, and we'll put some on."

I tilted my head back and listened to him talk as he applied it. He brushed it on, let it dry, did it again, and then let it dry again. When I felt my eyebrows, they felt crusty.

"Can you see it?" I asked.

Joe West looked at my eyes closely. "Naw," he said shaking his head. "When we get the Vaseline on it'll look like yah was sweatin'."

I felt it again. The reason Joe West was so concerned about holding my eyebrows together was because in one of my last amateur fights I suffered a long and angry cut over my left eye. It came from a butt, an accident Joe West didn't want to see happen again.

"This works, huh?" I asked, still feeling it.

"Yeah," he said and returned to rummaging around in the fight bag. Then a man came into our dressing room and held four gloves up in front of Joe West. Without saying a word, we chose the best two and the man left.

"Time for the gloves," Joe West said. "When yah get t'main events, we'll glove yah up in the ring. That way it gives time t'the people t'look yah over . . . place their bets."

He smiled as he spoke soothingly, and started to bend and twist the gloves.

"Why do you do that?" I asked.

"They're too stiff. Yah want 'em soft, so they fit yer hand perfect. That'll protect yer hand."

"But if they're not stiff . . ."

"The glove doesn't make yah punch hard. It's yer hand-wraps that hurt the other guy," he said. "C'mon, let's put 'em on."

Joe pushed the gloves over my hands and I helped him. Everything was moving toward the fight now; the crowd's screams were filtering down to our dressing room, the activity in the hallway was heightened, and my heart began beating faster.

"Move around now," Joe West said, holding still another jar. "I'll put this on just before we're ready t'go."

This time it was Vaseline petroleum jelly. Its duty was to protect my skin by allowing the punches to slide off without causing painful rashes and cuts. It also seals the heat inside your body, keeping you loose.

"It's about time," Joe West said.

"How can you tell?" I asked, not wanting things to be rushed.

"I can just tell," he said, applying the Vaseline to my face and shoulders. It was cold and sticky, like blood that's just starting to congeal.

A man knocked on the door and told us we were on. "Okay," Joe West said. "Touch my back and let me know yer always there. I'll lead yah up t'the ring."

He led me into the corridor again, up through the catacombs, up some steps, and around a corner. I saw the ring below me, glowing with a blue canvas some eighty feet away. "It's blue 'cuz the fights around here are televised," Joe West explained. "The white ones glare t'much."

I watched two fighters just stepping out of it. One was happy and one wasn't. As if by another signal, Joe West started for it. "Slice 'n' splice and take care a business," he said one more time. "Just listen t'me."

I followed him into the ring. Looking around, I saw some familiar show-biz faces like Robert Conrad, Michael Landon, and Shelley Berman scattered throughout the audience.

While everyone else was laughing and shouting, they remained calm, merely watching what was happening. I think it was because they knew of the tension, ego, and strain that performing takes out of a person. They understand the seriousness of performing.

My opponent stepped into the ring. He was thick-shouldered and thin-waisted. He was black and tall. His face was not natural either, but contorted with what I took to be hate. It was even worse than I imagined it would be. His manager had done a good psyche job on him.

Joe West saw me staring at him. "Just take care a business," he said. "Let 'em know right away who's boss."

The introductions came and went too quickly. The referee brought us together. He told us not to foul, to be gentlemen and sportsmen, and to always listen to him. I shot a glance at Joe West when he said that. He raised his eyebrows, saying in effect I should listen to him first, then the referee. We touched gloves and returned to our corners. Joe shook my hand before stepping out of the ring.

When the bell rang, it blasted away all of my thoughts. I was just reacting. I let my instincts lead me around the ring, ducking, blocking, and being careful. Then out of the crowd I heard Joe's melodic, soothing voice, "Counter 'em now," he shouted. "Lay back and counter 'em."

I saw a long left jab coming at my face. I ducked, stepping forward with my left foot. I felt his punch fly over my head and I cemented my eyes on his stomach. For that split second, he was totally unprotected. I jerked hard to my right, cocking my left arm in a tight hook. It slammed against his belly. He grunted, then tried to cover it up. I knew the fight was mine.

I stepped back a much more confident man. I knew what I was facing here, and it wasn't something supernatural. It was just a man. Prizefighters tell themselves that they can't possibly lose to men, only supermen.

"Slice 'n' splice," I heard Joe West say. Only a minute was left in the first round. It was as if I was the only one with that knowledge, and it made me powerful. It was my turn to go on the attack.

I jabbed, ripping through his defense, and shot a right hand at his face. They both landed, with the right hand smashing open his mouth. He reached out and tried to pull me into a clinch, but I ducked away, following up with a jab and another right hand. Not only did I want to win now, I wanted to knock him out.

"Take care a business," Joe West then said, and I smiled again. Ten seconds left, I told myself, and began making my way to the corner. Eight-nine-ten and then sit down. I hoped the stool was there. It was and Joe West was right behind it. It worked, I said to myself, watching my tall opponent walk across the ring.

"Aw'right," Joe West said calmly, holding my trunks away from my stomach, for unimpaired breathing. He removed my mouthpiece. "Yah done aw'right. Keep control."

I leaned to the right, hoping to see around Joe West to the other corner. "I think I hurt him, Joe," I said seriously. "In his body and head. I think I saw his mouth bleed a little. I think I can knock him out."

"Now just do what yer doin'," Joe West said, tilting a bottle to my lips. I gargled and spit it out.

I looked to each side of me, breathing hard. "I can get him, Joe. He grunted. I heard him grunt." My speech was fast and staccato.

"Just take it easy," Joe West said. "Yah learn more by goin' a couple a rounds."

"I saw him grunt, Joe," I said again.

"Aw'right, make him grunt a little more."

"I'm going to knock him out."

"Do what yah want," Joe West said. "Just don't get anxious. The man's scared, and that's the worst kinda fighter t'fight. Yah don't know what they're gonna do."

Then I breathed deep and sat back, feeling the ropes on my back. I looked up into Joe West's face. It was alive and excited. "Yah know something?" I said. "I hurt him in the head, right in the head!"

Joe West winked. "No kiddin'," he said grinning. "Now if yah wanna get back at that head, yer gonna hafta bring his arms down. Use that left hook to the belly again, but follow it with a right hand. Use three punches every time yah throw one."

I nodded and the ten-second buzzer alerted Joe West he had to get out of the ring. He replaced my mouthpiece and wiped more Vaseline over my eyebrows. "Aw'right, take yer time out there. Relax and look like yer enjoyin' yerself."

No need for that, I thought, I was enjoying myself. I had won the first round, and had the crowd on my side. That was important. When I could run my emotions through the crowd, and have them come back to me in the form of their clapping and screaming, it made me stronger.

The second round was like the first. I was learning to listen to Joe, and win the fight at the same time. I was combating the stifling fear that had inhibited my style as an amateur.

The next three rounds were like the first. I was just too fast, or scared, to be trapped and hurt. I won the decision, and when it came, Joe West simply patted my back and said, "Atta boy. We're on our way."

I paused in the ring, giving the crowd one last bow, but noticed they were all ignoring me now, talking about other things, and waiting yet, for the main event.

"C'mon, let's go," Joe West said.

He led me back to the dressing room. A few people shook my hand, telling me how good I looked. I believed them.

"I should have knocked him out, Joe," I said. "I had him a couple of times, but let him get away."

He nodded. "Yah weren't thinkin', man. T'knock someone out is rough. Yah gotta hit 'em with what they ain't expectin'. Yah gotta trick 'em inna doin' what yah want 'em t'do. Like in that third round . . . shit, man, yah had 'em, but yah let 'em get away. Yah let 'em know yah was comin' at 'em with a right hand. Yah shoulda faked it, and then hooked with yer left. The surprise knocks 'em out more 'n the punch."

Joe rubbed my back and smiled. "But yah won, and that's the most important thing. Yah just coulda done it more spectacular." The barren dressing room radiated a warmth now. Where before it had been nothing but a tough room for a prizefighter, it now stood as a victorious symbol of guts and pride.

"I feel good, Joe," I said bending my arms and rubbing my aching shoulders. "But I really feel dead."

"Course yah do. It's the tension. Man, I feel every punch yah get hit with, too."

Though I didn't see any abrasions on his face, I let it pass, and began undressing. I carefully folded up each piece of equipment and laid it out reverently alongside Joe's bag.

"Buy yah some Epsom salts tonight," Joe West said. "It'll pull the stiffness out."

Then Joe West heard the screams of the people again. He looked at me and said, "I'm gonna go up and watch some other prelims, see if I can scout an opponent. You be aw'right?"

I said I would and watched him leave. I showered slowly, letting the water run over my body and into my ears and mouth. I toweled off, pausing to talk to anyone who wanted to talk about my fight, and then went back and dressed.

When the screaming died, Joe West came back and handed me a bottle. "Here, this'll take that shit off yer eyes." It was nail polish remover.

We walked out of the arena together, without even watching the main event. I asked him if he wanted to see it and he shook his head. "I'm not a fight fan, Society," he said. "I've been around it too long."

His words puzzled me, and we walked through the large doors that we came in a couple of hours earlier. Joe West paused. "Ain't yah forgettin' somethin'?" he said.

I shrugged. "What?" I couldn't think of anything.

Joe West took my elbow and led me back into the building. We stopped at a window that had bars on it. "The money," I said, brightening up. Joe West winked.

I signed the release form and picked up my check for seventy-five dollars. "That's the difference," Joe West said pointing at the check. "Yah gettin' paid now. At least it'll buy yah some Epsom salts."

I shook my head. "No, I think I want to save this one, Joe. This is the first one. I want to remember it."

Joe West did a double take. "Well, take a picture of it then!" he said. "That seventy-five bucks'll come in handy. Aw, tell you what. I'll let yah have this one all t'yerself."

8

Denny Moyer

AFTER THAT FIRST FIGHT in Los Angeles, Joe and I hit the
road in his old station wagon. I fought every ten days or so,
in every town that would give us a fight. We fought the
local heroes just like he said we would, in their own back-
yards.

"Prizefighter gotta be a freewheeler," Joe said, still bearing down on the steering wheel that he never seemed to tire
of. It was now September, and I won eight more fights. I
was still undefeated.

The trips around the Southwest were amazing ones. We'd
drive places that didn't have fights, just to watch an opponent work out, to get a feel for him. In all of those fights,
Joe carefully explained what was happening. "Yer gonna be
fightin' a lotta styles around here," he'd say. "What yah gotta
do is figure 'em out, an' quick. One a these days you'll be
fightin' a guy with a lotta styles, an' you'll remember how
t'beat 'em. Use yer tactics!"

Joe West knew me better than any person alive. He was
my mother-trainer, taping my hands as well as holding
them, and my father-protector, too, always on the watch
over his young progeny. And he knew my moods; like the

time I wanted to be alone, or laugh, or when I needed a woman.

Those were the days that Joe West and I would burst into a town for a fight and he'd immediately begin handing out Xeroxed press releases about his coming juggernaut—Society Red. We were two men full of schemes and plans and dreams.

He was a masterful teacher during this stint. He never made demands of me, but he pushed and prodded and cajoled like the most facile of politicians. He had a form of reverse psychology that he used all the time, too. He'd never tell me to do anything, rather, just make it sound the best and easiest way to get where we both wanted to go.

There was a time when too many right hands were finding my chin. He shook his head as we drove home on a darkened freeway. "Man, rights is a fool's punch. They're easier t'get away from an' all of 'em. Man, they gotta travel twice as far across a guy's chest." Then he'd shake his head again. "Gettin' hits with rights. Just prolongs yer career. That's jus' not payin' attention."

That was true. When Joe West and I first got together, we were like stock market speculators. We wanted to get in and then get out. He knew I didn't want to be around it until I was stiff and sore each morning of my life.

So just that statement about getting hit with right hands prolonging my career made me imagine a thousand right hands coming at me. I would learn how to duck, counter, and block every one of them. Even in my sleep I would dream about punches coming at me, still blocking, countering, and ducking.

It was back in Los Angeles that I really learned about prizefighting. The competition, the ruthlessness of the opponents, and some of the real necessary elements. It was also the place that Joe West explained the art of punching hard and fast to me. His statements were carbon copies of Bearcat Baker's.

They both explained a punch in terms of a bullet striking a target. They showed me the barrel of a rifle, and how the grooves in it twist and rotate the shell for accuracy and power.

"Yah gotta twist it in there," Joe West would tell me. "Yah gotta fire from the shoulder and twist yer hand as it goes to the guy's chin. It's not the arm behind the punch, it's the shock and speed it gets there. Yah always wanna remember that. The fighters with muscles ain't punchers, they're weightlifters."

And to make everything easier, he invented names for the punches, with sounds that were to mimic how the punch was to sound. *Pop-pop-pop* meant the jabs. *Bam* meant the right hand. *Smack* was the left hook, and *whap-whap-whap* was any combination of them.

"Yah always wanna throw in combination," he'd advise. "Cuz if yah miss jus' one, that man gonna be fightin' back. If yah got three goin' in there, well, the chances 'r better of hittin' somethin'."

By late September it was time to go home, and we were both excited. The station wagon was packed up again, and headed north. We had planned to spend a solid year in Los Angeles, but my progress as a fighter was faster than either of us had expected. An indication of that was a rematch with my first opponent. I knocked him out in the second round.

Joe West was talking bigger fights and events. We even joked about fighting a certain top fighter. I laughed and related a story to Joe West about a Los Angeles fighter that I heard telling someone that he just got back from a bout with the guy and he was joking about what happened the night before the fight. He said two women came to visit him "and take the fight out of him."

Joe West didn't laugh. "Happens all the time," he nodded. "Yah get the opponent laid before a fight, and it works on his mind. He knows he been fuckin' around, not trainin'."

I scoffed at that. "Oh, bullshit, Joe. I've had women before fights."

"Well, just don't let me catch you," he scolded.

Once back in Seattle, Joe West and I kept at it. I moved back in with my folks, which made them happy, and even entered college again, taking some art and psychology courses.

But it was really prizefighting all the way. From the start of October 1968 to March of the next year, Joe West and I traveled the state. In that span of time I had seven more fights, winning them all. Now I was winning by knockouts. Out of those seven, five were KO's. And perhaps more importantly, they were ten-rounders, meaning that I was main event material. I was gloving up in the ring.

After a particularly good fight and win on March 11, 1969, where I decked my opponent in the second round, Joe led me back to the dressing room and became serious.

"What a yah think about havin' a big fight?"

I froze. It's what every prizefighter looks forward to, but dreads at the same time. "Moyer?" I said.

Joe West nodded, "Well . . ."

"Let's do it, Joe. I think we can beat him."

"With tactics," he winked.

The biggest fight of my life was set for May 1, 1969. Denny Moyer was the veteran middleweight who briefly held the light middleweight championship in the early 1960s. Now he was a full-fledged, ranked prizefighter, demanding his shot at the champion, Nino Benvenuti. He was a traveler and a contender, but also an old man by fight standards. It was the old man that I wanted to fight, the other things I wanted to be.

To train properly for the fight, Joe West and I hit the road for Los Angeles where they had more fighters to learn styles from. But that wasn't the only reason. Joe West was receiving a real bad press about matching me with a man with over a hundred fights behind him. He wanted to get me away from that so it wouldn't bother me.

"I want yah after them eyes," Joe West would tell me as I banged the heavy bag. "He got nothin' but scar tissue on 'em. Make 'em explode!"

I wanted that fight because Denny Moyer had been a boyhood hero of mine. Around the Northwest he was the closest thing to a real fighter we had to look up to.

But age and the road had taken a good deal of his skill from him. He had retired once to buy a tavern and build a family. But he must have just grown tired of it, because he was soon back plying the only trade he knew. When people talked of his comeback, he would smile and tell them he'd never been away. Denny Moyer was all of thirty.

"Yer only twenty-one," Joe West said to me, as we drove back to Seattle a week before the fight. "Yah gotta use it on 'em. Make 'em hustle after yah. Speed and movement."

There was a good buildup for the fight, despite the dire predictions that I was going to get my head beaten off. Everyone had their way to beat Moyer. Some said I should charge after him and try to knock him out. Others told me I was to box and be careful. And there were those who begged for me not to show up.

"Them eyes," Joe West whispered at the weigh-in.

I nodded and glanced at Denny Moyer's face where no hair grew because of old and deep scars.

"He was on the road this mornin', tryin' to make the weight, too," Joe West said, still whispering, as Denny

talked about fighting Nino Benvenuti after me. "An' the
bettin' line is only 2–1 against yah. Someone knows somethin'; it should be 10–1."

Joe West had reason to be happy with Denny's overweight
condition. He had structured the contract for it. It allowed
Moyer to weigh anything up to 163. Joe knew that if they
didn't have to come in below 160, they wouldn't train as
hard. I was lean and fast at 156½ pounds.

The fight got off to a quick start. I stalked Moyer and
went after those eyes. "He drops that left jab the way Louis
did with Smellin' in their first fight," Joe West told me in
the ring. "Go over it with a right hand to the eye."

I did and it started to redden. Then Moyer jabbed hard,
which made me duck low and inside. Our heads met for
the briefest of seconds and we parted. He stepped back with
a puzzled look on his face and pawed at his left eyebrow.
He said "shit" as he saw the blood on his glove. He knew
he was in trouble. Looking at him, he seemed much older
than thirty.

I kept attacking that eye. Between rounds Joe ordered,
"After that eye, man. Make it fall out!" He was ecstatic.

But Denny Moyer came after me hard, firing numbing
uppercuts that made my knees wobble. His boyish face was
desperate, standing atop an old man's body that had seen
too many cheap gyms and cheap meals.

The doctor stopped the fight after two rounds. Denny's
eye was raw hamburger by then. But I thought he deserved
a better fate. The record book would simply say I TKO'd
him. There would be nothing about a butt, or a controversy,
or anything.

I caught hold of Denny just as he was leaving the ring
and told him he could have a rematch. When he turned to
look at me I knew that our second fight would be no different. He had the tiredest eyes I had ever seen.

I told Joe West, who was screaming and bouncing around

the ring, that I wanted to give Denny a rematch. He looked at me as if I were nuts. "What for? He got what he deserved," he said.

But I thought Denny Moyer needed a second chance to postpone his own body's betrayal. No man can live with that, without a second chance to set the record book of time straight.

When the results hit the wire services, the wheels of prize-fighting began turning. I was stepping up and coming around to the top. A few more turns and I'd be there. One way or another.

9

Tune-ups

JOE WEST LEANED FORWARD on his long, low couch, dropping his head between his knees, reading and rereading the newspaper clippings of the Moyer fight. He had them all laid out before him on the floor, with the more favorable ones closer to him. The good ones he picked up and sent off in air-mail envelopes to his promoter friends around the country. He looked like a man counting his money.

"This'll make it for yah," he said handing me a most favorable one. "Make yah Society Red for real."

I sat across from him in a swivel chair, rotating from one side to the other. I shrugged and bent forward, taking it from his hand. Joe West watched me as I read it, waiting for my reaction.

It was a post-fight story about a kid with speed and flair, and how he incorporated both elements to annihilate the veteran Denny Moyer. I handed it back. "I don't like to read that crap, Joe."

"It's important stuff," he said, sounding almost hurt.

I swiveled my chair to face the large picture window. Mount Rainier was in the distance. Boats scattered on the lake drifted easily. "For you maybe," I said after a short pause. "It's a little self-indulgent for me."

"Self what?" Joe West asked, tilting an ear toward me.

"Indulgent," I said swinging back around to face him. "You know, like overeating."

"Oh," he nodded. "It gets yah fat."

I heard the basement door open, and steps on the stairs. Joe West perched forward and said, "Must be Martha."

"Where's she been?"

Joe West gave me a chagrined look. "Shoppin', man, spendin' all the money. Now yah watch this . . . she'll want me t'help her in with all the packages."

I smiled and waited. Martha was Joe West's wife of the last ten years. A beautiful-complexioned black woman with an electric smile and manner that I had liked instantly. When they had first gotten together, Joe West's hustle was golf. They blew into town together before Seattle's World's Fair, bought a house, and then began to figure out ways to pay for it. That's how Martha became Joe West's caddy.

"Papa [Martha's pet name for Joe] played this man for one solid week," Martha would laugh. "That's how we got the money for this place."

"Yeah," Joe West added. "That man just kept comin' back. Must a won close t'ten grand from 'em. I learned that from Charlie Sifford [one of the few touring black golfers] in Los Angeles. Yah gotta keep 'em comin' back."

Martha was always an independent woman herself. She was well educated and now taught school, pulling in the only steady money.

She breezed through the doorway and saw us, and smiled. "Papa . . . will yah help me in with some things I have in my car?"

Joe West winked at me. "Okay, baby," he said, without the slightest hint of sarcasm.

Martha and I talked for a moment, and when Joe West returned with the rest of the packages, she left the room. Joe West shook his head for a while, chuckling periodically, and then cleared his throat. "What'd I tell yah?"

"Right again," I smiled.

He nodded, and sat forward on his low couch again. "Now what we gotta do is figure out who t'fight next."

"I think we should go as fast as possible," I said.

"Anyone in mind?" he asked me.

"Top ten again? Another contender?" I said. "I don't care."

"What d'yah think about Fullmer?" He smiled after the question.

"Didn't he just lose to Nino Benvenuti?"

"Yeah, last December. Looked bad, too. Slow."

"He's strong, though," I said, qualifying it.

"His style's too set," Joe West countered. "He's easy t'figure out. Tactics."

I nodded. "Okay, Fullmer's fine with me."

Joe West smiled and reclined on the couch. "Fine, I talked t'Salt Lake City the other night. They want the fight."

I nodded again and smiled, knowing that Joe West had been taking care of business. "When?"

Joe West sat forward on the couch. "There's one problem. They want yah inna top ten a the world first. That way if yah beat 'em it wouldn't hurt."

I shrugged. "So? I just knocked out Moyer. He was top ten."

"They still might think yah a flash inna pan. Let's not rush into it blind. Now Fullmer's manager knows somebody in the World Boxin' Association, so if he wants the fight he'll get us rated. Yah gotta know someone in it t'get rated."

"Are you sure?"

"I'm never sure, but yah look at it with frequency an' probability. I talked t'him a lot in the last couple a days. He told me he wants the fight bad. When a guy wants somethin' bad enough, he'll do somethin' for yah. That sounds probable don't it?"

I nodded. "That sounds okay. But I don't think we should wait for Fullmer's manager before we make a move."

"Oh, we won't," Joe West said emphatically. "Yah gotta strike when the iron's hot."

"Who then? That puts us back at the same place."

"Not exactly. I been makin' a lotta phone calls, an' been gettin' a lot."

I shook my head and smiled. "Well, who then? Will you tell me?"

Joe West chuckled. "Don't get so excited. I know we gotta keep yah busy. I gotta guy in mind right now. A perfect opponent for yah."

"Who?" I asked.

"Guy named Polo Corona," Joe West answered. "He's fought every big middleweight inna business. They call him a taker, meanin' he gets hit t'much. Yah should handle 'em easy."

"Polo Corona?" I asked. "He sounds like an exotic cigar."

"But he's tough," Joe West said. "He'll go ten with yah. And right now, yah need more ten-round experience."

"Fine with me," I shrugged, not really wanting to fight an exotic cigar. "When?"

"Already got the date," Joe West smiled. "Couple a weeks from now. The twenty-sixth a May, in the Arena."

I stared at Joe West, knowing that he was at least two steps ahead of me. "Okay, fight's on then."

I fought Polo Corona and won every round. But it was an interesting night, for reasons that weren't to become clear until later. Just before my fight I watched a televised bout from Madison Square Garden involving the champion, Nino Benvenuti, and Dick Tiger. It was a nontitle affair that

Nino lost over ten rounds. The reason given for his loss was a broken right hand. Joe West and I both moved closer to the screen when we heard he had busted his right.

Fullmer's manager was present at my fight, too, to tell us that the date between his man and me was about set. To me that meant we were about to be rated by the World Boxing Association. I had already been rated by *Ring* magazine, as number eight man in the world, but that isn't the governing body of boxing, as far as title contenders are concerned. In my opinion, the W.B.A. is famous for stripping champions of their title for not defending it against their "prescribed" contenders. They're a very political group who enjoy doing favors for their friends.

The W.B.A. finally put me in the top ten, and to me that meant I was going to fight Fullmer. But Joe West didn't see it that way. "I wanna wait on that," he said. "I wanna gamble on somethin'."

I was perturbed. "Jesus, Joe. I don't want to fight more guys like Corona, I want to fight the big names. I think I'm ready for them."

He cleared his throat, and chose his words with precision. "Now, listen. I think we can hustle up a title fight if yah want."

"With Nino Benvenuti?" I said in disbelief.

"I think so . . ."

My mouth dropped. "Oh, come on," I said.

"No, now listen. It's a gamble, but one we can win. Yer rated by both groups, right?"

"Right."

"And when yah fought Moyer they were talkin' a givin' him the title fight. Well, yah beat 'em. Eliminated 'em."

"Right."

"And what'd we jus' see on television the night of the Corona fight?"

"Nino Benvenuti breaking his hand," I said. "And losing."

"Well that's it then," he said. "The W.B.A. is givin' 'em hell because they want t'see him defend his title against a real middleweight contender. They want a real title fight."

"Yeah, but they want him to fight Luis Rodriguez, who's the number one contender."

Joe West shook his head. "They won't fight Rodriguez until that hand a his is tested. And the W.B.A. won't let 'em fight anybody but a top tenner."

"I still don't understand what that has to do with us, Joe," I said.

"They're gonna wanna test that hand out on somebody."

"Me?" I asked incredulously.

"That's the gamble," Joe West said. "Yah know they gotta see yer name inna top ten there. And yah look the easiest outta all a 'em."

"Benvenuti, huh?" I whispered, beginning to realize that it was possible.

"Yah've seen 'em fight a lot, what d'yah think, what d'yah see?"

"An old man," I answered. "But a smart one."

Joe nodded, satisfied that the seed had been planted. "But we can't wait on that," he then said. "I want yah t'take a short rest, then come back t'the gym. We been goin' pretty steady for a solid year now without a rest. Besides, it'll give me time t'scout out this Benvenuti thing."

"Benvenuti, huh?" I said again. "Yeah, I'd like to fight him for the title."

I took a couple of weeks off from prizefighting, and tried to enjoy myself. But the title fight was constantly on my mind. So after that first rest in a year, Joe West and I got together to talk about Benvenuti and my next fight.

"I think we can get the fight with Benvenuti," Joe West said. "But it ain't sure yet. I do know we can't wait around for it. We gotta get yah some action."

"Good," I nodded. "I'm going nuts not doing anything. Anyone in mind?"

"Yeah, a guy from Fresno named Ted Lidgett. Supposed to be a good puncher. What d'yah think about 'em?"

"Okay, let's fight him then. You say he's a puncher?"

"Yeah, but my California scouts say yah can handle 'em."

On July 23, 1969, I knocked Lidgett out in three rounds. It was the perfect fight for me and Joe West. Between rounds we worked on tactics and talk. We worked as a team. Joe West told me that Lidgett dropped his hands for an instant as he stepped out of a clinch. "Hook 'em when yah step back," he said. "And come back with a right hand. Hit the chin."

I did just that and it all worked perfectly. Lidgett caught both punches on the chin and crumbled, felled by something he didn't even see. When he started to go down, I knew it was all over because he fell forward. When prizefighters drop that way, it means they were stumbling into the punch, and that's all she wrote.

And of course there was an incentive that stretched past this fight—the shot at Nino Benvenuti. I knew if I lost I would blow any chance of it.

The whole thing seemed far-fetched to me. I had only been a prizefighter a year, and though I was a ranked contender and still undefeated, I was hardly a household word.

"Take couple a days off," Joe told me. "Then we'll get somethin' in the fire."

I spent the time with two old college friends, Mike and Rich Condon, who had dropped out after the first year. It was odd being around people my own age again. I had to use different words and try to feel different things. But being with them gave me the opportunity to see just what I'd been doing since prizefighting became the biggest thing in my life. They kidded me a lot about being a violent dude in a time of peace marches and drugs, for taking money for the violence I created, and for being a mercenary for fat businessmen. I envied them in a way. I knew I had excluded a large part of learning by concentrating on one thing. I envied their freedom to march and protest, and to have unqualified fun.

They were twin brothers, one a rock musician, and the other a graphic artist. They had the same freewheeling attitude I did, though in reality we were at opposite ends of the world.

I was enjoying the sun and water at my folks' place. When Joe West called, I was stepping out of a slalom water ski, ending a good fast ride, and I jogged up to the house to take it.

Joe came right to the point, "How'd yah like t'fight the champ for the title?"

I laughed. "Sure, anytime. What else is new?"

"I'm not kiddin', man."

I took a deep breath and sat down in the wicker chair beside the phone. "What was that again?"

"The champ. How'd yah like t'fight Nino Benvenuti."

I was stunned. "Aww . . . I mean . . . what?"

"Just hop in yer car and get over here," he said, then paused and added "and drive careful, champ!"

I set the phone down and sat still in the chair. It wasn't possible I told myself. It couldn't be real.

"Who was that?" my mother asked.

"Oh, nobody," I answered, getting to my feet. I ran back down to the beach, told Mike and Rich I had to go, and left. I hopped into some new clothes I had bought, jumped in my Jaguar (also newly purchased), and drove to Joe's. He was waiting for me at the door. "Well, we got the fight. Half the gamble's over."

"Half?" I said.

He chuckled again. "Yeah, the other half is winnin' it."

Then he led me upstairs and explained the whole thing. I sat and listened carefully. I still couldn't believe it.

"Guy named Dewey Fragetta called," he said.

"Who's that?"

"Books fights all o'er the world," Joe replied, holding up his hand. "Now let me finish this in one sitting. We're supposed t'go back t'New York City next week."

"Want to fly?" I interrupted again.

"Now let me finish," he said smiling, though really eager to tell me. "We're t'meet a guy named Bruno Amaduzzi—"

"Who's that?"

"Will yah let me finish? He's the champ's manager. Now we're supposed t'meet him for negotiations."

When Joe said negotiations, he puffed up with pride and importance. "What about?" I asked again, foolishly.

"About the fight," he answered.

"Then it's really on."

Joe West shook his head. "That's what I'm tryin' t'tell yah. Some things gotta be worked out. It sounds pretty rushed. Yah still wanna fight Benvenuti?"

"Damn right, Joe. I've been thinking about it. I can beat him, I know it."

"Good," he said, bobbing his head.

"Where do they want the fight?"

"Will yah let me finish?" he said, dropping his arms down to his sides. "Now they want us there next week, so pack a bag and we'll leave Monday or Tuesday."

"Let's fly, huh?"

Joe West shook his head. "I don't like t'fly, yah know that. Let's drive."

I nodded, then said, "Well, where do they want the fight?"

He screwed his face up. "Rome or Naples, in Italy."

That broke me up. "And you don't like to fly?"

"Yeah, I might not let yah fight 'em if we gotta fly over there."

"Bullshit," I said. "We're fighting this guy and winning it."

Joe West smiled. "Okay, it look like this team hits the road again."

"To New York City anyway," I smiled.

"The drive back'll be good," Joe said. "We got a lot t'talk about if we're fightin' for the title."

"Like what?" I asked.

"It's a total different scene," he said. "There's more involved . . . but there's plenty a time for that, just pack yer bags. Oh, and another thing, don't tell no one about this. They wanted it all kept secret."

"Okay," I said, thinking that to be a strange request.

"But on the road again," Joe West said.

"And this time it's first class," I said.

Joe West shook his head. "That's the only way we've gone. Just 'cause we're fightin' for the title don't make it first class. People are either first class or they ain't. The title don't make it nothin' but a bigger fight."

10

New York

"YAH DID WHAT?" Joe West asked as he started his car for the long trip to New York.

"Invited a couple of friends along. Their dad lives in New York," I said.

"This isn't a fun trip, man," he frowned. "It's business. It's on the road."

"They just wanted a ride."

Joe West was mad. All I had done was invite Mike and Rich to ride along with us to New York. I didn't think it would be that big a deal. Joe did.

It was a rough ride back East and Joe West pulled it straight through, with but a few hours of sleep on the side of freeways and in empty parking lots. And it was the first time that I saw Joe West visibly tire. I remembered his words, "Ain't shit t'be on the road all yer life." He was proving his own point.

Reaching New York City, we dropped Mike and Rich off at their father's and checked into a downtown hotel. I told them I would be getting in touch as soon as I knew what was going on.

Joe West made some phone calls upon our arrival, and

set everything up. We were to meet Bruno Amaduzzi the next morning in the hotel lobby. Bruno would call us when he was ready.

The next morning as I was shaving, I heard the phone ring. Joe West picked it up and talked for a few minutes. Then I heard him hang it up. "Yah about ready?" he asked.

I pulled the blade across my face, watching myself speak. "Just about."

"Well, c'mon, we don't wanna keep 'em waitin'."

I washed the razor out in the sink and dried my face with a towel. "What's this guy Bruno look like, Joe?" I walked out of the bathroom and pulled a velour turtleneck over my head.

"Dunno," Joe West said, sitting next to the phone, looking out the window.

"How will we find him then?"

"He'll find us," Joe West said, blinking away his thoughts and pulling himself out of the chair. "C'mon, we gotta go down inna lobby."

We walked out of the room to the elevator. Joe West stepped in and pushed the L button. "How should I act, Joe?" I asked. "Like a tough guy?"

He shook his head and leaned against the wall. "Jus' be yerself. Yah meet the same people goin' down inna fight game yah met goin' up."

"You do, huh?" I smiled.

Joe winked. "Yeah, c'mon." He pointed to some chairs to the right and told me to sit down and wait. He then checked the place thoroughly before sitting alongside of me. "Guess he's not here yet," he said.

"He'll find us," I nodded.

Joe picked up a newspaper. He peered over it to the entrance of the lobby. Then a large man with sunglasses entered the room. He had a thick chest and olive-oil complexion, which contrasted nicely with his short brown hair. He glanced around once, saw us, and peeled his sunglasses off. Then he fixed both Joe and I with the most remarkable smile I'd ever seen. It was a wide beam that created little dimples in his puffy cheeks.

Joe West immediately got to his feet and said, "Now if that ain't him . . ." then walked over and introduced himself and me. It was Bruno Amaduzzi.

He looked at me and vigorously shook my hand. He lifted his arms and opened them. "Like my son," he said clearly.

I want to be a tough guy, I say to myself, and here he is calling me his son. Shit. Then another remarkable thing happened. I watched a complete transformation in Joe West. No longer was he a blunt man with hardened speech. I saw a man standing there with polish, poise, and dignity. Every word he used was chosen perfectly for the occasion. There were words I had never heard from Joe either. I asked him about it later and he shook it off.

"I know the words. I jus' like t'use things that's more comfortable. An' besides, this Amaduzzi was probably expectin' some country nigger," Joe West laughed. "An' I like t'shake people up with things they don't expect. That's one thing yah wanna do in fightin'. Aw'ways hit 'em with what they don't expect."

Bruno Amaduzzi then took us to lunch, where he and Joe talked prizefighting like a couple of kids comparing stories. I merely sat off to the side listening, still amazed at Joe West's polish, and trying to look like Errol Flynn.

When the check for lunch came, Joe West grabbed it. But then Bruno grabbed Joe West's arm and prevented him from reaching into his pocket. Joe stared at him hard. Bruno became red from embarrassment, and removed his hand. Joe West glanced at me and winked, dropping his hand to his hip pocket where his knife "Henry" sat. Bruno finally talked Joe West out of the check and we all shook hands again. Then Bruno Amaduzzi hailed himself a taxicab and left.

"What did he say?" I asked Joe quickly.

"He's gotta set up the contracts. We'll meet 'em tomorrow."

"Where?"

Joe West lifted a piece of paper with an address on it. "Here. This is it, Society. We're gonna get it." Then Joe West burst into his familiar chuckle. We laughed together.

The next day we took a cab to the midtown address Bruno had given Joe. Bruno met us at the door. Once in the apartment, we were introduced to Mrs. Scaravel, a fortyish blonde, who was Bruno's lawyer. She clutched a manila folder of papers and set them down on the kitchen table. The room was bright and cheery, with a great view of the East River.

Joe West and I stared at her as she sashayed around the room in a flowing, yellow Pucci gown. It was the same color as her hair, which was pulled back stiffly on top until it dropped to her shoulders in streamy, long curls.

We all took seats around the table, Joe and I with our backs to the window, Bruno and Mrs. Scaravel facing us.

"There are two contracts here," Mrs. Scaravel began. "One in English, and one in Italian. Do either of you know Italian?"

"A little," I said.

"Okay," Mrs. Scaravel said, watching the brief exchange of glances between Joe West and I. "If you have any questions, be sure to ask them." Then she began going over the multipage contract point by point. There were a lot of little clauses that I had to initial, and I did, as Joe watched. One main point said that if I should fall out of the international rankings, the fight contract would be void. The various boxing bodies were pressuring Nino to defend his title against a top contender, preferably Luis Rodriguez, the number one man. If Nino fought anything but a fifteen-round title fight, they would threaten to take his title away. So if I fell out of the top ten, it couldn't be a legitimate title fight.

Finally we had everything settled. Bruno rose from the table quickly and shook my hand. Everyone started talking fast and excitedly. Then Bruno invited Joe West and me out to his favorite Italian restaurant in New York. We had a feast of snails and pasta, to celebrate the contract signing. The meal was excellent. The sentiments expressed were warm. But my stomach felt a little queasy—I was going to fight the champ.

11

Friends

We stayed in New York a week after signing the contracts, but it did not turn out to be a happy time. Originally, we planned to stay only one day. The hotel had parked Joe West's car on the street, anticipating an early departure. When we went out to fetch the car that morning, we found someone had done a hit-and-run number on it to the tune of five hundred dollars. We spent a week waiting to have it repaired.

During that extra week, Joe kept to himself. Mike, Rich, and I discovered Manhattan, especially Greenwich Village. Though I was still working out every day in a New York fight gym, the evenings were mine. But Joe and I shared the same room and that brought us to a head a couple of times.

"That you, Society?" Joe West called from out of the darkness. It was late. He had been sitting there with the lights out waiting for me.

"It's me," I said tiptoeing in the room.

"Where yah been?"

I faced the direction of his voice. "Out to a show," I answered. "Had a few beers with Mike and Rich."

I didn't hear anything from him so I started to undress. Then Joe struck a match and its light flashed around the room. He touched it to his cigarette. I looked at Joe, his face was bronzed and tight.

"Hadn't ought t'be fuckin' around," he said icily. "Yer fightin' for the title yah know."

"Two months," I said, undressing.

He drew heavily and exhaled loudly. It sounded like he sighed at the same time. "Yah oughta get somethin' straight here," he said. "If yah wanna go drink beer and play wid yer friends, yah shoulda stayed in college. Yer a fighter now, and yah gotta act like one. A fighter needs his rest, man."

I lay down on my bed. I could see his cigarette burning red across the room. "I'm used to getting home this late, Joe." I propped myself onto my side, leaning my head on my hand and elbow, facing him.

He shook his head. "Yer fightin' for the title, man. That means yah can't be one a the guys. Yer in a tough business and yah gotta be tough. Anytime a prizefighter starts t'fuck around his instincts go on vacation."

"I wasn't fucking around," I answered sarcastically.

"Yah were laughin' and stuff," he said. "Yah can't be that loose. I seen yah with 'em, an' it ain't good."

"They're just friends."

"Friends shmenz. When yer fuckin' around yer not thinkin' about the fight. Listen, a prizefighter got one friend an' that's his manager. This 'I gotta be me' shit don't get it. It's we gotta be *we*. Don't forget how yah got here."

I shrugged. "You brought me."

He gave me a quick glance and a frown. "No, here to New York and a title fight. Don't forget what got it s'quick. It was dedication."

"So I'm still dedicated," I said.

"It's not the same. When a prizefighter get t'fuckin' around and enjoyin' hisself, he's nothin' but a side-show performer. Yah gotta be a fighter t'be a fighter."

"Look, I just had a few beers with a couple of friends of mine. That doesn't mean anything but what it is."

"I don't mind yah drinkin' a beer or two," Joe West said. "But it's late an' yah need yer rest. Win the title before yah start messin' with yer friends again. Just remember the way yah got here."

"I'm remembering," I said, flopping onto my back. "I'm remembering everything about Los Angeles and all those fights."

"And on the road," Joe added.

A few days later we were on the road back to Seattle. The only souvenir I had brought with me was a small harmonica that I was just beginning to learn to play. I opened the glove compartment, set up my sheet music, and started blowing and sucking notes. Joe flinched everytime I hit a wrong one.

"Gimme a break, man," he said, pointing at the harmonica.

I kept blowing and then held it aside. "Joe, by the time we hit Chicago, I'll be what Casals was to the cello."

"In tune?" he winced.

The road home was an easier one. Joe West wasn't obsessed with getting across the country in two and a half days. Every night we would find a nice motel and bed down tranquilly. I suspected the reason might be because Mike and Rich weren't with us. Also the fight details had been settled.

"What'd the New York hotel cost you?" I asked.

"Close t'two hundred bucks," Joe West said. "But I'm not payin' 'em. It was their fault my car was wrecked."

The first day after leaving New York City, after we had had a good night's sleep, I rose early to get in two miles of roadwork. As I was jogging along the edge of the road, I stepped into a hole and twisted an ankle. I limped back to the room and concealed it from Joe West. But when we were set to leave again, he noticed my difficulty getting into the car.

"What's wrong, man?" he asked, starting up the car.

"Nothing," I said. "Just twisted it a little."

But then it began throbbing, and causing me great discomfort. Joe West watched me and the road carefully. His face held genuine concern.

"How is it really?" he asked again.

I shrugged. "I can't walk on it too well."

"How'd yah do it?"

"Stepped in a hole on the road."

He gave me a tight-mouthed look. "I've told yah t'be careful. Just try t'stay off it until we get back home then. We can't afford t'postpone the fight. Just take it easy."

We drove for awhile and my leg still gave me problems. Doubt began to set in, causing my head to work overtime in worry. It was the first such injury I had ever experienced, and I didn't know what to expect.

"Why couldn't we postpone it?" I asked.

He turned his head from one side to the other, slowly. "Take this for what it's worth, man," Joe West said. "But there might be some bullshit happening here. I've seen it before, an' this smells the same."

"What kind of bullshit?" I asked.

"Well, they might be plannin' on givin' yah the title. An' then winnin' it back."

I frowned and tightened my eyebrows, looking directly at Joe West. "What?"

He nodded. "I'll tell yah, that foreign scene a boxin' is

vigorous. It's just like it was in this country around the thirties, forties, and fifties. The best fighters aren't the top contenders, nor the champion."

"What?" I said again. "The champ's the best because he's champ. They're not going to give me anything."

Figure it out. I seen it before. The only way a really old fighter or good fighter can make money is by tradin' off the title, and winnin' it back. It used t'happen all a time, until they was exposed."

I still stared open-mouthed at Joe. He was serious.

"Joe, I can't believe you've got your head screwed on straight. Where the hell do you come off talking like that?"

"This is the way I see it. They know Benvenuti's through. He's old, fat, and been fuckin' around." With that word, he glanced at me, and then continued. "An' the name a the game is money. They can get more by fightin' as a challenger. Now yer an unknown, but when yah beat Benvenuti you'll be made. The people in Italy will fight t'get tickets for the re-match. You'll fill that damn stadium again. And that's the name of this game, Society."

"It's all bullshit," I said.

Joe West nodded. "I don't know, man. Where there's smoke, there's fire. These people are used t'gettin' what they want."

"Meaning?"

"Why d'yah think Angelo Dundee called me up in New York when the contract signin' leaked out?" Joe West asked later.

"I don't know, to congratulate you for doing a good managing job?"

Joe West smiled, making me feel terribly naive. "He thinks yer gonna win it, an' would like t'get a fight with yah for Luis Rodriguez, his fighter."

I remembered standing next to Joe in New York when the call came. He talked for awhile, politely, and then said good-bye. I asked him who it was, and he casually mentioned it was THE Angelo Dundee, manager and trainer of Muhammad Ali, Carmine Basilio, Luis Rodriguez, Willie Pastrano, and Jimmy Ellis.

"What did he say?" I remember asking.

"He congratulated me on your progress," Joe West smiled broadly. "He thought his fighter deserved it, but he told me it's a good move."

"Rodriguez does deserve it," I said.

Joe West laughed and sat down in the hotel chair. "Shit, he doesn't deserve another chance at it. He's fought for more titles 'n yah got fingers. Besides, he's like Benvenuti—old. I'd let yah fight Rodriguez tomorrow."

I watched the road, still remembering and flashing back. Then I smiled, remembering how happy Joe West was when Dundee called. It signified something to him. That he had joined a select few in the boxing world that could move a fighter from a nobody to a contender. Gil Clancy of New York could have done it, and so could have the late Yank Durham, Joe Frazier's manager. That was indeed select company. Joe West knew it and loved it. He had arrived.

"You'd let me fight Rodriguez, huh?" I asked, glancing from the road to Joe West's face.

"Like I said in New York, man. Tomorrow."

When we pulled into Seattle, we weren't as tired as when we hit New York. Joe West dropped me off at the end of my driveway. "Take a couple a days off, rest the leg, an' then come on down t'the gym. Be prepared to fight the toughest fight yah ever fought. Prepare t'die t'win it," he said seriously.

"You're something else," I said. "Three days ago you said they were going to give it to me, and now you tell me to be ready to die for it."

"Just coverin' all bases, man," he guffawed.

12

Rome

Joe West gazed out the Boeing 707's window, watching the airplane taxi to a halt at Rome International Airport. His face was tight and his fingers drummed a nervous tune on the seat's armrest. "Looks like they was expectin' yah," he said, smiling, the first time he had done so since leaving Seattle some fifteen hours ago.

"What?" I answered, seeing him angle his head to the window. I looked out and saw a dozen newsmen scrambling toward the portable staircase that was being wheeled to the rear exit of the plane. They had cameras slung over their shoulders like assaulting troops landing on a beach. "I'll bet they don't even recognize me," I said.

"Bottle a wine says they do," Joe West answered. "They know what yah look like, that yah got red hair. They can put two an' two together."

The rest of the passengers noticed the commotion outside the plane. "Must be a politician," one said.

Another agreed. "Or someone very important. Look at all those cameras." Everyone cast questioning glances around the airplane for the mysterious celebrity.

Martha, Joe West's wife who had made the trip with us,

listened to the other passengers and laughed. "They just don't know, do they?"

"Is it a bet?" Joe West asked again.

"Bottle of wine it is then," I said.

Joe West smirked. "Payoff the fourth a October then, after the fight!" Then he saw the passengers on the plane begin to stand and fumble with their coats. "Come, let's go. Comb yer hair a little an' let's get out there."

"Don't say anything to them," I whispered as I stood up. I looked at my cowboy boots, and straightened my silver belt buckle with the longhorn steer on it.

"I won't," Joe West said, stepping in the exiting stream of passengers who were still buzzing about the "celebrity."

Before reaching the rear exit, I tapped Joe West on the shoulder and asked him how I looked. "Do I look like a cowboy?"

"A cowboy?" he said, stopping in his tracks, holding up the flow of people.

"Yeah. I read where Nino Benvenuti did a spaghetti western a while ago. I'm going to tell everyone I'm gunning for him."

He raised his eyebrows and broke into a smile. "Aw'right Tex. What are you gonna tell 'em? That the fight'll be high noon for 'em?"

I grinned. The passengers behind us grumbled about our holding up the line. I gave Joe a shove and we walked to the door. He bent through it and walked easily down the staircase. I followed him, but paused for a moment at the top, giving the newsmen every chance to recognize me. They didn't and I quickly skipped down, even bumping into one of them at the base of the stairs. I said I was sorry and walked to the bus that was to take us to customs. The reporters were still clustered at the exit stairs.

"Bardolino," I said to Joe West, falling into the seat beside him.

"Ciao," Joe West answered, exhausting his repertoire of Italian. "You win again."

The reporters began looking at one another. A stewardess told them all the passengers were off. They walked toward our bus. The passengers were still buzzing about the "celebrity."

The bus driver was told whom they were looking for. "The fighter to fight Benvenuti." A drunk steeped in swill and courage then said, "I'll fight Ben—Venuti."

"Better get on up there," Joe West said to me. Before I could answer, I heard a tapping on my window. I looked down. It was the reporter I had bumped into. He was motioning me out frantically. The jig was up; I had arrived.

"Give 'em what they wanna see," Joe West urged. "Go on . . ."

I looked again and all the other reporters were scrambling to the bus's main door. "You come with me, huh?" I said to Joe.

We got up and walked to the front of the bus. "That's him, that's Frazier?" someone said aloud, obviously thinking of Joe Frazier, the heavyweight.

"I thought he was a Negro."

"It might be the guy behind the kid," another answered. "The tall black one."

"He's too thin," I heard someone reply.

"Fighters are deceptive," an authority claimed. By this time I had reached the front of the bus, and was grinning broadly. I nodded at the driver and hopped off the bus, making my fist a pistol and pointing it at everyone.

"I'm gunning for Nino," I said. "October 4 is high noon for the champ."

They lifted their cameras quickly and pushed forward, clicking their shutters. They ate it up. Then they had a brilliant idea. I was to reenter the plane and exit again. That

way the reporters and cameramen would be off the hook
for missing me the first time.

"C'mon now," Joe West advised. "Let's not keep the other
people waitin'. Let's not hold up the bus."

The bus drove us to customs where we were met by the
copromoter of the fight, Reno Tommassi. "Come, we have
cars waiting for you." He pointed out the terminal doors and
I saw a half dozen small foreign cars with garish, yellow
fight posters pasted on them. The reporters dashed for the
trailing cars in the convoy as Joe West and I got into the
lead one. The car burnt rubber as it left the airport, and the
rest of the cars squeeled into the street following us.

"I don't want my fighter runnin' around promotin' this
thing," Joe West said. "I want 'em t'rest."

Reno glanced at Joe and smiled, and then removed it as
fast as it appeared. "Everything is all taken care of," he
said.

Joe West lit a cigarette and inhaled heavily, watching the
scenery flash by. The road to Rome was flat and lined with
old, dead trees and patches of long grass that swayed in the
wind. We entered the city, a sandy monochromatic red. The
people on the streets were alerted to our impending passage
by a constant cacophony of horn honking from our entire
entourage. They jumped to the safety of the sidewalks.

We skidded to a halt in front of an old, stately-looking
hotel. Reno jumped out, barked orders at everyone, and
shook hands of more people. The other cars then came
squealing in. The reporters piled out, talked to Reno, and
waited.

"When do we get t'Naples," Joe West asked Reno, as the
bags were being taken to the hotel room. "I want my fighter
t'train."

Reno shrugged. "Mmm, one day, two days . . ."

"One day," Joe West said definitively, then he motioned
toward the hotel. "C'mon, Martha'll have the rooms ready."

"I have my own room?"

"Yah don't think I'd let yah stay with Martha an' me? Besides, after New York I think it's better that we don't keep the same ones. Yah got different hours 'en me, an' it's better to be by yerself . . . get that knack a survivin'."

Two hours later we were back in the streets of Rome, heading for a press conference. It was another fast ride that often found Joe and myself alternately squashed against each other and the car's doors.

We were not prepared for the sight that greeted us: a crowd of people filling up two blocks, all pushing and tugging at the arrival of Society Red. We squeezed out of the car and they began chanting, "Capelli de carrota, capelli de carrota . . ." They charged forward for autographs.

"What are they sayin'?" Joe asked.

"They're calling me 'carrot head,' or something like that," I said, bumping my way through the mob. Reno led us to the table at the front of the room. Fifty reporters pressed closer. Then Bruno Amaduzzi entered the room. He was the stand-in for Nino who was still training at his Mediterranean camp. He walked over to me and shook my hand and playfully slapped me in the stomach.

"He's seein' what kinda shape yer in," Joe West said, whispering in my ear. "It's an old-timer's trick. They can feel what kinda shape a guy's in."

I hardened my stomach and tried to look solid.

After brief introductions and speeches from everyone at the head table, I was told to stand and answer the questions posed to me from the floor. The Italian press embraced every ideological strain in the country. Each sect had its own house organ. There were communist papers, socialist papers, capitalist papers, fascist papers, and government papers. The communist paper hated Nino,and the fascist paper hated the communists because they hated Nino. They even tried to bait me a few times.

The one thing they all had in common, however, was drink. A table full of half-empty bottles attested to that.

Reno translated the questions for me and I fielded them with ease. I even played a little harmonica to keep everybody loose. Then one questioner asked me about my credentials as a bona fide challenger. He pointed out I had fought only seventeen times and beaten only one contender. And that fight, against Moyer, had been stopped by a cut.

Before I could answer the man, Reno got to his feet and halted the proceedings, saying we were tired from a long flight and had to rest. The reporters grumbled and left. Bruno Amaduzzi shook both of Joe West's hands and then kissed him. He did the same to me.

"How yah feelin'?" Joe West asked me as we motored back to the hotel. His eyes were wide and he seemed to be really enjoying himself.

"Good, Joe. I have to think I'm a fortunate kid for all of this to have happened so fast."

Joe West thought for a minute, and shook his head slowly, as if he were fitting the pieces of a puzzle together. "Yep. You are. But don't forget, yah worked hard for it. Hard work aw'ways pays fer itself. That's why I want yah t'start trainin' tomorrow again. I don't wanna leave nothin' t'chance."

13

Naples

We took our training camp to Naples, a dream city for me. It is a bawdy, seaport city, full of gamblers and hustlers and loose, fast-talking women.

The days of training preceding the title fight were also exciting. I was super-energized all the time. Everywhere I went there would be a crowd following me. But as the fight drew nearer, I had to struggle hard to escape all that. Joe had told me many times a fighter has to conquer himself before he can hope to battle someone else. At times I would sneak out and walk the streets alone.

Most of my thoughts centered on Nino Benvenuti. Everything I did was with Nino Benvenuti in mind. My hotel room had Nino Benvenuti pictures pasted on the walls. And one that was special to me I kept on my night stand, next to my pillow. It was a commercial that he had done for an ocean liner company. He was smiling a toothy grin over a plate of spaghetti, and a half-empty bottle of wine stood next to him. It was a large picture of him, and I memorized that face a thousand times. Every abrasion, every scar, every blemish was cemented in my mind. Anything about him that could give me a clue I remembered. I even shadowboxed that picture each night before I went to bed. Staring deep into his eyes, I let him know I was going to try to kill him.

I only saw Nino once during my training period in Naples. That was at a restaurant where a prefight dinner was held. Our respective tables and entourages were separated by a thin screen. I kept looking in his direction, hoping to get a glimpse of him drinking more wine. Joe West saw me watching his table and chuckled.

"What's he doing over there?" I asked Joe. I didn't want to get caught by Nino looking over there. That would have given him a psychological edge. I wanted to appear indifferent.

Joe West looked over and dropped his mouth. "Oh, no, you wouldn't believe it," he said in wonderment.

"What, what! Tell me."

"He's eatin'," Joe West replied laughing. "With a knife an' a fork. Jus' like you or me."

A fighter looks to establish a certain rhythm in his training camp. It's a kind of a yin/yang thing. He wants his mind to be just as ready as his body. If one of them gets there first he knows he's in trouble.

The night before the fight I knew I had to get my head together. There was a large and beautiful mountain in Naples that overlooked the sea and the city. So after dinner I had the chauffeur take Joe and me to the lookout point. We rode in silence. The air was crisp and clean. A slight breeze was blowing off the water. Everything was peaceful, soothing; I felt comforted. I walked over to a low stone wall and placed my foot on it. Joe West thoughtfully followed me and did the same.

"Yah come a long way, Society," he said. He lit a cigarette and exhaled.

I didn't say anything; I was more interested in surveying the lights of the city that lay below us. Then I trained my attention on the sea. It was dark and difficult to see, but I became hypnotized by its motion that I saw in my mind's eye. Sooner or later my thoughts made their way back to Nino. What was he doing? Was he thinking of me at the same time I was thinking of him? I sensed he could feel my thoughts about him.

"People just don't know what being a fighter is all about, do they?" I said to Joe West.

"Naw, they lay their money down onna day a the fight an' then go home after. They never see a fighter fightin' hisself every day he's trainin', gettin' ready for that one night."

I smiled. "They don't know what they're missing."

"Yes they do," Joe West said slowly. "All they wanna see is entertainment. They jus' don't care about what it takes t'get there . . . the travelin' and all that trainin'. Half a the people don't even know what goes on in promotin' a fight. Like I said, they jus' don't care. It's too bad."

"Well, I wish I could think of fighting as entertainment still," I nodded. "But it's too damn painful to be."

"When yah turned pro, yah shoulda realized that," Joe West said, flicking cigarette ashes into the air. "Ain't no recreation. It's business. Why do yah think I tell yah t'take care a business when that bell rings? It's because that's what it is. Yer business is yer fists, mine's takin' 'em to where we can take care a it."

I sighed, inhaling the Mediterranean air. A million lights flickered below us like drunk fireflies, darting and weaving through the city.

I bent over and picked a few stones off the sidewalk and tossed them slowly over the bank. Joe watched me and kept drawing on his cigarette. It was a quiet time and one that meant a great deal to us. We had climbed this mountain together.

I breathed deeply one more time and let it out. "What say we head back to the hotel?"

Joe West snubbed out the cigarette and nodded. We walked back to the car and returned to the hotel. It was getting late and I was tired. I had big things to do tomorrow —win the middleweight championship of the world.

"See yah inna mornin'," Joe West winked, slapping me gently on my back.

I closed my door and stripped to my shorts. I walked to the windows and slid them open, revealing the street. Then I glanced at Nino Benvenuti's pictures and started throwing slow punches at them, all the while talking to myself.

After about a half hour of this, there was a gentle tapping on my door. I walked over to it and pulled it open about eight inches. Two small, almond-shaped eyes looked up to me and smiled. Then a larger pair stepped from the side and asked to come in.

I opened the door and smiled. They walked in and stood in the center of the room, gazing around. My thoughts went back to the story I had heard in California from the fighter who had said that two girls, prostitutes, were sent to take the fight out of him. I laughed to myself. That was old-time thinking if ever there was such a thing.

"What can I do for you?" I asked the larger one. She threw her head back and smiled. A hardened look told me what she could do for me.

Then the two girls exchanged glances quickly. They heard something.

"Hey, Society," Joe West said, rapping on my door. The girls looked panic-stricken and I held a finger to my lips, showing them to the bathroom. To cover their giggling, I turned on the water faucet.

"Yeah?" I said to Joe West, opening the door a crack.

"Lemme read one a yer books yah got."

I hesitated for a second and opened the door. I listened

hard for the sounds from the bathroom but all I heard was rushing water.

Walking to the suitcase then, I spied a pair of women's shoes, which I kicked under the bed. "Poetry? Comics? What? . . ."

"Gimme some poetry."

I grinned. "My name is Red from Society, I come to fight and to rioty . . ."

Joe West laughed. "Not that, gimme a book a it." I did and he thumbed through it.

"Yer not gonna have t'read this are yah? If yah have to, then tell me."

I smiled, knowing Joe West to be extra careful in not upsetting my plans for anything. "No," I said. "I don't think I'll have to."

"Okay . . ." Joe West said, walking back out of the room. Then he stopped, and said, "An' I need some toothpaste. Yah got any?"

I thought he made a motion to the bathroom door and I frantically picked a book up and called him over to it. "Hey! Look at this one, will you. It's great . . ."

He took it and I slipped into the bathroom to find one girl standing in the shower with her eyes open wide, and the other sitting on the toilet seat. They both held their hands over their mouths.

"Here," I said closing the door again, handing Joe West some toothpaste.

"Thanks, see yah tomorrow."

I nodded and closed the door behind him. I spun around quickly and thought about the two women, leaning my back against the door. They peeked around the bathroom door and smiled.

"What are you doing here?" I asked.

The small, almond-eyed girl walked to me. Her pointed breasts danced slowly beneath a silky, soft paisley dress. She began to smile. As she got closer and closer, her pearl-white teeth made themselves clear. She stood close to me and looked down, and her black hair fell forward as her friend unzippered her dress. She reached out to me, putting her hand on my waist, and slowly dropped it to my crotch.

I smiled and grabbed her elbows, pulling her close to me.

14

The Weigh-In

I WAS UP EARLY. Sitting alone in the large, empty hotel restaurant, I sipped espresso and thought about the fight and the morning's weigh-in. It was going to be my first meeting with Nino Benvenuti.

Joe West joined me. His clothes were stylish and bright, from his alligator shoes to his green-yellow sport jacket. "G'mornin' Society," he said seriously. "How'd yah sleep?"

"Good," I answered, tilting my head forward.

"I see yah drinkin' a little coffee there," he nodded at my cup. "Yer weight good enough t'drink some liquid?"

"About 159," I said taking another sip.

Joe nodded quickly and took a chair across from me. "That's damn good weight then, that's punchin' weight." As he said that he flexed his arm and felt it. His eyes remained fixed on the coffee cup I held in my hand. He'd never seen me drink it before.

But my weight perked him up. Joe West knew that the plans for the fight hinged on it. For Denny Moyer he had wanted me to be light and fast; now he wanted to have more bulk and strength behind each punch. So for this fight he wanted me three pounds heavier.

"Yah'll beat this guy inna body," he reminded me again. "An' 159 means yah punch harder, not that yah sacrificed no speed. Yer still just a kid with growin' t'do yet."

"I'm twenty-one," I said, snapping at him.

"Relax, relax," Joe said easily.

The site of the weigh-in was the Hotel Mediterraneo, about a five-minute ride from where we were staying. During the short trip, Joe ventured, "I'll bet yah Nino's havin' trouble makin' the weight."

"Why do you say that?" I said.

"I saw 'em eatin' at that restaurant," Joe West said looking out the window. "An' he was puttin' it away. Drinkin' that wine an' shit. I just think he's takin' yah easy. That's good 'cuz after three rounds he'll begin t'tire."

"We'll see," I answered.

"Yeah. But remember, anything over 159 for him is dead weight."

I nodded and watched the driver weave in and out of thick traffic. When we reached the hotel, the entrance was packed with reporters and fans. They were pushing and tugging against each other, and when they saw my car pull up they surged toward it. A few security men tried to hold them back.

"Careful out there," Joe West said, as I stepped out of the car. "Don't be shakin' no hands."

I entered the crowd and they encircled me, pushing forward with their cameras and microphones. I answered the nagging questions about the fight from habit now, knowing that anything I said would be past tense before they could print it.

A little kid ran up to me and said that Nino Benvenuti was already inside attired in a sweat suit. I motioned Joe over to me. "He tells me Nino is upstairs sweating and exercising," I said. Joe West raised his eyebrows. I started for the elevator doors, pushing the crowd out of my way. "Come on, let's go up," I told Joe.

The kid had been right. Nino was walking around in the sunlight of the veranda. His forehead was beaded with sweat and he pulled his arms back and forth across his chest. He looked at me and walked away to the back room, muttering to himself.

"Looks like yah mighta upset the champ," Joe West chuckled. He winked at me and grinned. "Hadn't oughta do that."

The room filled quickly with reporters and fans.

"I'm glad t'see it's sunny out," Joe said. "That's a good sign. I dreamt last night it'd be a good day for us."

"Oh?" I answered casually, watching the activity of all the people gathering around the scales.

"Yeah, I knew if we could see Vesuvius today, it'd be a good night for us. I always have these kinda thoughts before good nights."

I looked at Vesuvius myself, and saw a possible rain cloud off to the left. "What if it rains?"

He shrugged. "Signs is always adjustable, Society. That's what's good about 'em."

Joe West was like a fighter with his superstitions. He was a knocker-on-wood, a tosser of salt over his shoulder, and a horoscope reader. He might have picked it up from another fighter of his he had told me about. That fighter firmly believed that if they were driving to the fight, and were stopped by a red light, they'd lose for sure. That put a lot of pressure on Joe West as driver. It also gave him the idea that signs, however ridiculous, had to be adjustable.

Then Joe West pointed to the scales. "Better go inna back there," he said, handing me a bag full of equipment. "An' get dressed. They look about t'begin."

After stripping my clothes off and slipping velvet trunks on, I reentered the main room. The cameras started attacking me again, and I tried to look around them to where the officials were gathered to announce the weights of each fighter as he stepped on and off. I walked straight into Nino, bumping his arm.

We shook hands and Nino greeted me in broken English. I tried to greet him in Italian. This was a moment of kinship for us. We briefly looked into each other's eyes, knowing all too well what the other man was going through. Most people in professional careers can spot fellow protagonists. Prostitutes can, writers can, and so can prizefighters. When faced by the mirrored image of yourself in someone else, his eyes reflect your own feelings.

I scanned Nino Benvenuti's face, looking for some physical or psychic weakness. I saw none. It was a small face, with heavy eyebrows and a not so gentle nose. The nose resembled putty that had been bent and twisted around, and then straightened out again. It wasn't wrong for a fighter to look like that. It was his badge.

They called for me then, and Joe West came to my side. I glanced around and stepped up on the scale. An official slid the weight bar forward and balanced it. He called out a metric measurement and the crowd hushed. Joe West fingered a metric measurement chart.

"Good weight, about 159. A little over, but good," Joe West smiled. I smiled too and paused for a minute on the scales to allow more pictures to be taken. Then Benvenuti and I traded places, again looking at each other's eyes. Mine must have looked happy because his looked concerned.

Nino stepped on quickly and then back off to the side. I didn't hear them announce the weight and neither did Joe West. "What was it," he asked me quickly. I shrugged. Then he raised his finger and hollered, "Una momento, una momento," in clumsy Italian.

He walked to the scales, grabbed a towel, and wiped the weight bar off. "Weigh 'em again," he demanded.

He wiped the bar off because one of our handlers told us that oftentimes, the fight managers would alter their fighter's weight by placing a stick of chewing gum on the bar. That way nothing over 160 could register. Joe West really didn't understand the principle. But with the title on the line, he wasn't about to take any chances.

So when they reweighed Nino and he came in at 160¼ pounds Joe West began complaining about the extra quarter pound. Nino stood on the scales watching, and then dropped his hands to his trunks, pulling the elastic band out and letting them snap back. He was saying in effect that it was his trunks that were overweight. Joe West smiled at him and let it pass. He leaned over to me and whispered, "He's over 159, Society. Dead weight."

Then an Italian television announcer came up to me with an interpreter. He explained that Nino and I were going to be interviewed on live T.V. He was going to ask me two questions now, and have me give my answers to the interpreter, so that when the camera was on it would appear he understood everything I was going to say. I gave him my answers to the two questions and he thanked me. Just as he left, the interpreter, a serious, short-haired man, looked at me and stressed, "Now remember the questions. One, how do you feel? And two, how are you going to do tonight?" I said I'd remember.

When they brought Nino in, the director raised his hand and we were on. The announcer smugly sauntered over to me and spit out the two questions. He spoke them so fast I wasn't sure whether this was the thing we had rehearsed or not. I squinted and then turned to Nino. "What did he say?"

The announcer became gripped with the fear that he was losing his job. Sweat broke out on his forehead. I watched Nino think over what was asked, and say to me, "He wants to know . . . how you do tonight." His arms were raised up and out with expression.

"Oh," I said simply. "Tell him that I will probably knock you out."

Nino stared at me for a second and then straightened his back, explaining what I said. The crowd laughed. They loved it: Nino telling everyone how I was going to knock him out.

Nino and I shook hands and headed in opposite directions. The weigh-in was over.

"Let's go, huh?" I said to Joe West.

"Aw'right," he said, rubbing my back.

We ate, took a long walk along the Mediterranean, and then returned to the hotel. We were silent. As I opened the door to my room, Joe West asked, "Anything I can do for yah?"

I shook my head. There wasn't anything he could do now. It was again, the lonely territory of the fistfighter. I was confident, excited, proud, anxious, and alone. Just like I would be in the ring tonight.

We nodded at each other and I turned and entered my room. I walked to the suitcase and lifted a book out of it, and laid down on the bed. Opening it randomly to the middle, I started reading. The pages looked blank.

15

Against Nino for the Title

"How yah feelin'?" Joe asked, as we prepared to leave for the stadium.

"Just fine," I answered.

"Get any sleep?"

"About this much," I said, raising my hand and holding my thumb and forefinger about an inch apart.

"Aw'right, that's good. C'mon, everyone's waitin' inna car below." He pirouetted and led me downstairs to the car. I sat in the back with Joe. Martha sat in the front next to the driver.

The ride to the Stadio S. Paolo was a long one. I didn't talk so neither did anyone else.

Joe West started to light up a cigarette to kill time, but I turned my head and leveled him with a baleful stare. He then picked it out of his mouth and placed in on the ashtray. Without saying a word I looked back out the window.

Then I unrolled the window, sticking my hand out. "It's cold out there, Joe."

Everyone heard me speak and turned their heads to me, agreeing.

Joe West nodded, "That's good. This bein' a outdoor

fight'll be good for you and bad for Nino. Old muscles don't limber up inna cold like young ones."

I bobbed my head and looked back out the window, shutting off conversation again. Joe nudged me. "There's the stadium." His voice was full of respect and a little nervous.

I looked out his window and saw it. A large concrete structure, circular in shape lit by dozens of searchlights. Long, dark shadows smothered the many people milling around the outer gates. My body became electric.

"Looks good," I said.

"It is good," Joe said, still staring at it.

"More signs?" I asked.

Joe West looked at me and nodded. "Ain't missed a light yet an' it don't look like it's gonna rain."

The crowd grew bigger as we got closer. Joe then cleared his throat and turned toward me. "Yah know, it's been two months since we signed the contracts for this thing." I nodded, and then he added, "Two months and fifty-odd years," in a subdued, almost inaudible tone.

The driver let Joe and me off at the fighters' entrance. The people surrounding the area recognized us. But they didn't rush or charge us. Rather they just pointed and whispered with respect. It made me feel pretty important.

We walked past a pair of tight-lipped security guards, down a long, dark corridor to the dressing room. The noises outside became muffled, and I listened to the tune Joe West whistled. When we came to a large door, Joe pushed it open and gazed inside. He motioned me in.

"Grab a seat there," he said, pointing at a padded rubbing table. "We got a lotta time yet."

Joe hung my robe and trunks on an overhead pipe that crossed the room. They dangled on the hanger like a mobile and cast an eerie shadow on the facing wall. He began removing equipment from the bag.

"I'm going to the bathroom," I said, hopping down off the table.

Joe West looked up and to my left. "It's over there."

I found it and a full-length mirror, which prompted me to begin throwing punches at my shadow. I moved closer to it, and then bent forward to examine my face. I began squeezing what I thought was a pimple. I told myself that I had to pick this reluctant blemish or I'd lose the fight. The pimple turned out to be a stubble of hair from my two-days' growth of beard. I always liked to grow beards before I fought. I thought it made me look meaner and tougher.

"What are yah doin' there?" Joe West asked, entering the bathroom.

I pulled away from the mirror, startled. "Nothing."

He looked at my cheek and its red blotch. "What the hell's that?"

"Ahh, I was picking a pimple and it turned out to be beard," I said sheepishly, rubbing it.

"Well, don't rub it for chrissake," he said disappointedly. "Go back an' sit down. We don't need no self-inflicted wounds."

I returned to the padded table and watched Joe West fumble with the handwraps. He muttered the whole time. "Toughest fight a my life an' he's inna back there beatin' on hisself," he mumbled. Then he shot me a sideways glance and shook his head. "Chrissake, Society, don't give 'em no help. We don't need no cuts from pimple-pickin'. That's all they need here is a little blood, an' they'll stop the fight for sure an' give it t'Amaduzzi."

"You mean Nino, don't you?"

He sneered again. "One's as good as the other."

Just as I was fighting Nino Benvenuti in the ring, Joe would be taking on Bruno Amaduzzi.

"Don't forget," he said, seriously. "We ain't gonna get no

My fight against Denny Moyer on March 22, 1969 was the biggest of my career to date. (Top left) Moyer connects with a left to the chin. (Top right) He sets to counter the same punch from me. (Bottom) I've opened the cut over his eye that's going to cost him the fight.

(Above) I've just knocked out Ted Lidgett in a Benvenuti tune-up.

(Opposite page, top) In this May 1969 fight I've got Polo Corona on the ropes. I took a unanimous 10-round decision from him.

(Opposite page, bottom) Here Corona is ducking away from a left hook, but he's got nowhere to hide.

(Above) Stalking the champ: Nino Benvenuti. He waits anxiously as I close in. I lost the fight by disqualification in the sixth round.

(Below) I've just landed a left in our October 22, 1969 battle for the title.

(Above) Benvenuti closes in, but I'm upright and ready for his flurry.

(Below) Nino takes a breath before moving in, giving me time to get set.

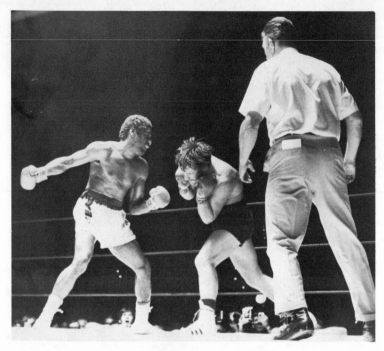

(Above) Against Luis Rodriguez in August 1971. Here comes his sucker punch.

(Below) Rodriguez had a sixth sense about knowing when to pull back from a right hand.

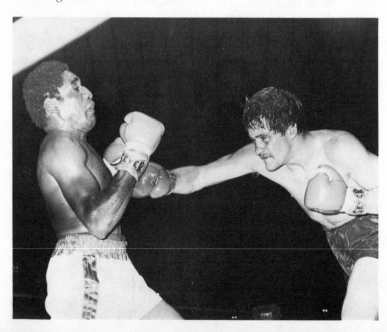

(Top left) He won the fight because I wasn't freewheeling that night, but I got my licks in as this photo shows.

(Top right) An exchange between Mike Pusateri and myself in March 1972.

(Below) The jab is the punch to throw when you're in doubt about what to throw.

(Top left) I could see Pusateri's left coming a mile away. I'm pulling back and ready to drop in a right at the same time.

(Left) Joe West puts Vaseline on a cut over my right eye. It helps congeal the blood.

(Below) A reflective moment: Joe West and myself.

help from the referee. If anyone does, it'll be them. They tell me this guy is Amaduzzi's ref."

I shrugged, "Once the fight's going, there's not much he can do. A referee is a referee."

Joe West grunted something that I didn't catch, but it didn't sound like something in favor of my statement. I knew that he was really concerned about the choice of referee. That to him was the most important part to a fight. He told me that a good referee will let a fight set its own pace, and that when the good ones are doing their job, you don't even know they're there.

Joe West liked ex-fighters for referees. "They know what a fight is," he said. "They let yah fight."

Joe West then told me that the referee tonight was to be Tony Gilardi, a man who had not refereed a fight in six years. But I scoffed at his concern. I didn't think the referee could make a difference.

Then Paul, a hometown journalist and friend who had come down to our dressing room, asked me about the tensions in a title fight. I told him they were considerable. We talked for awhile until Joe cleared his throat. I looked at him and he tossed my shoes and protective cup at me. I caught all of it and he smiled.

"That's a good sign," he said.

"What is?"

"That yah caught the gear. That's about nine onna scale a ten."

"Yeah?" I said, sorting out the socks from the shoes. "What's ten then?"

He chuckled. "When yah hear the ref say it over Nino's body!"

That loosened us all up a little and we laughed together. A short, heavy-set man entered our room. "You about ready?" he asked Joe West.

Joe looked at me and told me to be ready when he got back. "Where are you going?" I asked.

He nodded toward the stranger. "Gotta go watch 'em wrap Nino's hands." Then he winked. "Make sure they don't wrap inna roll a quarters."

The stranger was Al Silvanni, the American trainer of Nino Benvenuti and sometime actor in boxing films. He was also a good friend of Frank Sinatra, who was rumored to be part of Nino's managerial trust. The papers had hinted that Old Blue Eyes would be at the fight tonight.

"Be ready t'wrap yer hands when I get back," Joe West said just before he left.

Paul and I talked a little bit more as I finished tying my shoes and getting into my protective cup and trunks. When Joe West returned, I was ready. He pointed to a chair, and I sat in it. Al Silvanni returned with Joe West and stood to my left as Joe carefully wrapped my hands. All the while they talked about things that didn't have anything to do with the fight. That disturbed me a little, and I wondered how they could be so calm about this whole thing. I sure wasn't. The tension seemed to be feeding on the little time I had left.

Then Joe slapped my hands, signaling that he was done. I stood up and Al Silvanni removed a pen from his shirt pocket and carefully drew an X across each bandage. Then he wished us luck and left. I heard his footsteps echo down the hall.

"Why the X?" I said.

"So we don't unwrap 'em an' put somethin' in, an' then rewrap 'em," Joe West answered. "Like a sticka dynamite." That made him chuckle.

"It's just an X," I said. "It looks like it could be copied."

"Nooo," Joe West said. "A man knows his X like he knows his face. Yah don't mess with the X's inna fight game."

I listened to this great truth and nodded, watching Joe

gather himself together for his usual prefight story that was supposed to loosen me up. He didn't disappoint me.

"Remember when you wrapped in that three-inch wooden dowel under yer handwraps?" Joe West said through a smile. "An' yah were inna ring an' the ref walked over to check yer handwraps?"

I remembered it and smiled. "Yeah. I was watching you when he came over and said he wanted to check them. You turned away and said, 'Oh, shit.' "

Joe nodded, knowing he had me going. "And he felt yer knuckle an' that piece a wood, and yah said it was to protect yer knuckle, and then the ref nodded his head an' said it was OKAY because it was UNDER the knuckle!"

"I couldn't believe it," I smiled, shaking my head.

"Shoulda wrapped inna horseshoe," Joe West then laughed. And I laughed with him, loosening up.

"How yah feelin'?" Joe asked, checking his watch.

"Good," I said.

"Well yah better start gettin' looser," he instructed. "Are yah nervous at all?"

"A little," I said.

"Nothin' t'be nervous about," he said. "It's just like all the others."

"I was nervous before all those, too."

Joe West nodded and looked away. "Well it's not exactly like the others, it's better."

"So's the nervousness," I grinned.

Our eyes met for a moment. We both had the same feelings now, that we had done everything right and that we deserved to be here. I was remembering we had only been together a little over a year and now I was fighting for the championship.

"Aw'right," Joe said. "Now let's get it straight what we're gonna do inna fight. Yah gotta roughhouse 'em from the beginnin'. Don't give 'em no rest. Make 'em punch at yah.

Don't let 'em control the fight. If yah do that he'll pick yah t'death with that jab. An' when he starts t'throw that upper-cut, level 'em with yer hook."

"Right." The pressure began building again.

"Good. This is what's gonna happen then. We're gonna walk t'the ring behind our flag. We'll enter the ring, listen t'each national anthem, come together at center ring, an' then the fight'll be on. It'll happen quick, s'be prepared for Nino's rush."

Then a man entered our dressing room with the gloves we were to use. Joe West looked at them and asked, "I thought we were gonna put 'em on inna ring?"

The man explained that Bruno Amaduzzi wanted to do it in the dressing rooms. Joe West nodded and took them. "That Amaduzzi's smart," he said. "He don't want his fighter standin' out there inna cold. An' I was gonna stall puttin' these things on yah."

"Jesus, they're small gloves, Joe," I said, helping him push them on.

"Six ouncers," he said. "Not the usual eights."

"These could hurt somebody," I said feeling the thin pad-ding covering the knuckles.

"That's the idea," Joe West nodded, winding the tape around the glove. "Now let me grease yah up."

He covered my body and face with Vaseline, so the punches wouldn't scrape my skin. Then our call to the ring came.

"Aw'right, here we go. I know yer ready, I can smell it. Jus' be cool in there, an' remember: TAKE IT TO HIM!"

We started for the ring. My heart danced down the long corridor. Brief flashes of light struck at my eyes, and I hunched my shoulders up and down, trying to get looser. Then we saw an armed honor guard, holding our flag. I straightened my back and fell in behind them. We took a couple of steps and entered the stadium.

I first noticed the ring. It looked far away, canopied by light, surrounded by countless people. My eyes roamed to the bleachers. I was struck by the fact that everyone had set newspapers on fire next to them, to keep warm from the chilly October night. They told me 40,000 people were here. I held back a gasp.

"Here we go," Joe West said, noticing that I looked dumbfounded. He gave me a gentle push.

The trail to the ring went right through the ringside seats. Guards had cordoned off a small area leading to it. As I walked toward it, spectators bent over and pounded my back and shoulders, hollering. But I could only hear what was in my own head. Jab, duck, punch, smack!

As I got closer to the ring, the faces squeezed in even closer. I looked at all of them and their intense expressions, and then back at the ring that was getting closer and larger. I didn't feel like I was walking. I was floating, with absolutely no control over my legs.

Then there was a flurry of activity in front of me, and Joe West bounced up the steps to the ring and held the ropes open. When he looked back at me, I followed him up, hoping to God that I could look graceful, hoping to God I wouldn't trip. When I made it up I bent down and swung into the ring, letting fly three quick punches into the air.

That's when I first began to hear it. It was so low and far away at first, I didn't think I heard it at all. But it grew louder and louder, gathering momentum like a sea wave until, it seemed, someone hit the volume switch and a thundering, tumultuous cheer hit my ears. It was deafening, and at the same time the ringside cameras began popping their flashbulbs. I could have been in an air raid. I threw three more punches, thinking that they were cheering for me.

"Nino's coming," Joe West said, leaning over to my ear so I could hear him. "Jus' ignore 'em. Go over there and rub yer feet inna rosin for traction."

I did, and out of the corner of my eye I saw Nino enter to the crowd's pleasure. They hollered, "Neeno-Neeno-Neeno!" I kicked my feet into the chunks of rosin and felt them crackle under my feet.

I walked back to my corner to see Joe checking out the crowd. "There's Martha an' Ernesto an' company," he said. "Wave at 'em."

I looked over the crowd briefly and saw them. At last I didn't feel so lonely. There were friendly faces out there after all. And when they jumped to their feet, screaming, it was as if they were the only ones there because I heard every word they said.

"Careful now," Joe West quickly whispered. "Here comes the ref. Be polite."

I looked up and saw a short, plump, balding man walk toward me with a scowl on his face. I started to greet him when he snatched the towel out of Joe's hands, and roughly wiped the Vaseline off my face and body. Then he grunted something at both of us. Joe West and I looked at each other in surprise.

"Okay, here's the national anthem," Joe West said. "Stand tall."

We listened to the strained sound of the rough rendition, and then it was abruptly halted. "Oh, oh," Joe West said. "Looks like we're in trouble, they cut it short."

I couldn't tell whether he was joking or not, so I ignored it. A little thing like that wasn't going to bother me.

"Let's listen t'theirs now," Joe West said.

We did and they hit every note perfect. Then the ring was immediately cleared out by the referee and Bruno Amaduzzi, who wanted to get this thing going, not wanting his fighter standing too long in the cold. The referee murmured instructions at both of us, and then we touched gloves.

I tried to find Nino's eyes but he wouldn't look at me. I

was screaming the whole time, "Look at me! I'm going to get you!" But no one heard me.

Joe West led me back to the corner and grabbed my hand, before he hustled out of the ring. "Shake my hand an' take care a business," he said. I nodded that I would.

I turned in my corner and faced Nino Benvenuti, waiting for the bell. I waited and waited and waited. Come on, I screamed in my head. Come ON! COME ON! The wait was incredible, though in retrospect I don't think it was more than a few seconds. But when you've played a scene in your head for as long as I had played this one, it can really drag if you can't execute it.

The bell. I sighed in relief. But that sigh was short-lived. Nino Benvenuti walked straight across the ring and threw a wide left hook at my head. Duck, I screamed at myself. Too late, my blurred vision told me. It hurt bad.

No, no, no, I screamed again, imagining myself falling. Nino still came forward, all the while throwing punishing punches as I retreated. The plan was now set. He was out for a fast kill. I had to back up. Get out of his way—fast. Panic set in.

Then I stopped in my tracks and saw another hook coming. This is it, I told myself, I'm not going back anymore. I ducked under the punch and swung with everything I had. I hit mostly air. But the referee waved his arms and separated Nino and I, slapping his forehead at the same time he frowned at me.

"What?" I heard Joe West scream from the corner. Out of the corner of my eye I saw an official berate him for "coaching from the corner."

I looked at the referee in amazement. "What did I do?" He frowned again and motioned us to resume the fight. Nino did just that, in a total abandonment of the cautious, graceful style that had won him the championship. He struck at me with fencepost punches, often breaking through my guard. I tasted blood in my mouth and was again reminded of its warmth and not so unpleasant taste. It's a bitter contradiction.

Then I felt Joe West telling me that the round was almost over, using the signals that had been introduced in my first professional fight. "Take care a business," said his voice.

I tried to move to my corner, understanding that only ten seconds were left of round one. I wanted to, needed to, sit down quickly and think this out. But Nino Benvenuti made it difficult. Everything I did, he reacted against. The bell finally rang and I found my corner.

Joe West leapt through the ropes and removed my mouthpiece. "Well, yah just went a round with the champ," he said, as if that would make the bruises less painful.

"What the hell is the referee saying?" I asked, breathing in and out heavily. I sat forward and propped my elbows on my knees. Joe West reached for my beltline and pulled my trunks away from my stomach so I could breathe.

"Yah can't duck here," was Joe West's answer.

"Can't what?" I said in surprise.

"Duck," Joe West said simply. "They like that fuckin' Olympic stand-up style. They know that's the thing Nino won the gold medal with."

I shook my head. "I don't get it, I don't know what you mean."

"They're accusin' yah a buttin' 'em, or tryin' to."

"We haven't touched heads!"

"Don't make no difference," Joe West replied sharply, glancing quickly at the hawk-faced referee. "When they accuse, it's as good as sayin'."

"Who won that round?" I then asked, grabbing Joe's hand that held the mouthpiece, replacing it in my mouth.

"He had the edge."

"Put some Vaseline on my face," I said quickly, hearing the buzzer that told the corner men to exit the ring.

"Ain't got time," he said, glancing at the referee watching us closely. "Next round." Joe West bent through the ropes and out of the ring. "Aw'right," he said at the bell. "Go after 'em."

I walked out determined to fight him differently. This time I was going to go after him. I did, ducking low and firing hard, clumsy punches to his sweaty midsection. He grunted and pulled into a clinch, where he began hitting the back of my neck with his thumb and fist.

"That's an illegal punch," Joe West screamed, only to be warned again about coaching from the corner.

I struggled to muffle his arms and grabbed his elbows, neutralizing them. Then I saw a man in a way that only a prizefighter can see one. Nino's eyes were wide and his mouth tight, wired together with discipline and fury. He moved his gloves at me hypnotizingly, like a snake charmer with his flute.

I remembered seeing that hungry look before, but not in the ring. I'd seen it on cats, lean and hungry ones. I'd seen that look in the young hustler's eye, as it travels the length of your body probing for weaknesses. And I'd seen the look in prisons, when I would box exhibitions. I'd see it when I left the walls, past the clanking doors and turning keys. It's a look to remember.

Then Nino went at my face again, only to find me ducking below his punch, countering with increasingly effective punches to his body. He grabbed me and we clinched for a moment. During this moment he complained openly to the referee about my ducking. I didn't blame him. It's tougher to hit someone when they duck. The bell ended the round.

"Yah went another round with the champ," Joe West said quickly, removing my mouthpiece before I could sit down. "Yah got a little blood in yer mouth."

"I don't want to hear it," I snarled, spitting to the side.

I didn't either. Blood is only something to talk about when it's on the other guy.

"Keep takin' it to 'em," Joe said. "Peas porridge hot!"

"What do you mean?" I asked, trying to look around him to see what Nino Benvenuti was doing.

"Stick t'the ribs out there," he chuckled, starting to loosen up. "He's gettin' tired."

"From hitting me," I said through a loud exhale. I inhaled deeply, then exhaled again.

"That's aw'right. Yer takin' everythin' he has. He's yers in four more rounds."

"What round is this?" I asked.

"Three comin' up."

The buzzer came again and Joe West left the ring, replacing my mouthpiece. At the bell, I walked out and stood in front of Nino waiting. But there seemed to be a change now. He was not so tall, in fact, was bent over and hunched down a bit. I smiled to myself, hoping that this meant I was getting to him. But he quickly threw two hard punches at me, a long jab with a straight right hand behind it. I leaned to my left, avoiding the jab, and then bobbed my head even lower, coming up as fast as I went down. The right hand passed over my head and I felt good having avoided the punches.

But the referee started slapping his head again, berating me for ducking. He was getting more and more serious. I looked over at Joe West. He waved his arm, indicating I should attack.

I pinned Nino against the ropes and banged his stomach hard, with alternating lefts and rights. By now he had a pained expression on his face and a mouth full of complaints for the referee.

"Bullshit!" I said out loud, listening to another complaint, and growing tired of it. He looked at me amazed, as if I wasn't supposed to talk. Then he clinched me again. Moving his left arm up to my face, he tried to jam his thumb "inadvertently" into my eye. Now I had him, I thought. When a guy has to resort to tricks, I know I've got him.

But I soon began to respect the number of tricks this guy had. He could punch, rabbit-punch, kidney-punch, hit low, and use his thumbs, all the while looking like a nice guy. He was a magician in that ring.

But it still meant to me that he was getting desperate. At the end of Round Three, I told Joe West about it. He agreed. "It's yer fight now," he said. "He's tirin' bad."

"I'm tired myself," I breathed loudly.

"But yah don't look it," Joe West said. "That's what's important."

"Four coming up?" I asked, beginning to relax a little.

"Yep. Now's the time yah take it t'em hard. Once burnt, lesson learnt."

I looked into his eyes again, asking for an explanation. He shrugged. "Well, now yah know that yah can't stand back and play with this guy. Yah gotta roughhouse 'em."

I bit into the mouthpiece, strengthening my determination. Round four, five, and six began to go my way. I could see and feel it in Nino's punches, as well as I could my own. His became wider and heavier to throw and were usually preceded by small grunts and sounds of fatigue. I was tired too, but strong, full of the confidence one can muster when he knows victory is in the offing.

In the break between round six and seven, Joe West was ecstatic. "Yah got 'em now, Society," he said proudly. "Did yah see Amaduzzi help Nino back t'the corner?"

"After we tripped and fell?" I said, remembering the awkward moment that Nino's and my legs became entangled, depositing both of us on the canvas.

"Around there," Joe West answered. "But Amaduzzi

jumped inna ring and grabbed Nino by the waist and helped 'em to the stool. He's dead. Yah got 'em. This fight ain't goin' three more rounds."

When the buzzer sounded for the exit of the corner men, Joe replaced my mouthpiece and smiled, winking. "Go after 'em . . . champ."

I charged out at the bell and quickly confronted Nino at center ring. He moved around tightly, with his eyes fixed hard into mine. Then he struck at me. I ducked quickly and moved into his body. But before I had the chance to land my punches, I saw the referee frowning once again. Then he started waving his hands, shaking his head. I stared at him. They were stopping the fight. I thought for a moment they were going to raise my hand.

I'm champ, I said to myself.

Then Joe West started screaming. His words weren't clear but his bitterness was unmistakable. I watched the ring immediately fill up with people I didn't know, and they all slapped Nino Benvenuti on the back.

"What happened, Joe?" I looked around blankly.

He held my robe in his arms like he was cradling an infant, and shook his head. "They gave it t'Benvenuti."

"Why?"

"Duckin'," Joe said. "They said yah was duckin' and buttin'."

"We never touched heads . . ." I replied numbly. I didn't know why I wasn't crying, screaming, or still fighting.

"I know it," Joe replied.

"It's horseshit, Joe. If you can't duck then it's not fighting, it's masochism."

Joe West could do nothing but shrug.

"I had him, Joe," I pleaded, as if it would make a difference.

"They took it away from yah," Joe West commiserated.

"They sure didn't give it to us," I said, bringing up the

subject that we had discussed after the New York contract signing.

"They stole it away," Joe West muttered, dazedly. "Let's get outta here."

Then I heard the boos from the people. It was incredible. Panic seemed to break out at ringside, and I heard, "Fix, fix, fix," being shouted by the people milling around.

Guards surrounded Joe West and me, and led us through the screaming mob. But they didn't try to strike me; they wanted to comfort me. That made me feel better.

My dressing room was packed with people apologizing and explaining. I couldn't listen, but felt I had to maintain a stoic presence.

"It's all right," I shrugged many times. "I just wish I could have looked better."

Joe West heard me. "What are yah talkin' about? Yah fought jus' like yah had to. That's how yah beat a guy like that."

"Not tonight it wasn't," I remarked.

"You were the champ tonight, man."

"But he'll be the champ tomorrow," I philosophized.

The United States Secretary of Transportation, John Volpe, was there, and entered my dressing room. He told me I had fought a good fight, also mentioning that the ending was very strange. I ran out of things to say to everyone. Joe West just stood around shaking his head, doing his best to console himself as well as me.

When the dressing room cleared, and I finally took my shower, it hit. I had lost. That hurt deeply. And the way I lost magnified the hurt. Benvenuti hadn't beat me, the referee had. An old man merely waving his arms. Joe's fears had been prophetic.

Joe West and I left the arena alone.

"Joe, I'm sorry. Maybe I could have hated him a little bit more?"

He shook his head and waved away my words. "Ain't got nothin' t'do with it," he said slowly. "Difference a opinion don't make for fights any more. It's money."

We met our driver at the fighters' entrance. Joe West paused before stepping into the car and looked back to the stadium, the place that was to have been the repository of the grand and glorious triumph of Society Red.

It was only a month after the Nino Benvenuti title fight that I fought again, winning a ten-round decision over someone I should have knocked out. I did four months in the army reserves and after my release fought again, winning another ten-round decision. I was still ranked in the top ten. I wanted a rematch with Benvenuti. Joe said he was working on it.

What I got instead was another offer to fight Denny Moyer. I said I'd take it. But just before the Moyer fight, I agreed to fight Mario Marquez, a local club fighter in California. Joe West didn't want me to have two ten rounders inside of ten days, but I talked him into it. "I'll be careful so I won't get sore hands or cut," I told him.

But I was too careful and Marquez took the decision from me in ten rounds.

"Prizefighters can't be careful," Joe West told me. "They gotta freewheel."

But I had the rematch scheduled with Denny Moyer, who was also still ranked in the top ten. I knew if I beat him, that losing fight in California would be erased. I beat Moyer, stopping him on cuts again in the eighth round. In all, a strong, relaxing fight. I was a contender again, now the number two challenger in the world.

"Get me Benvenuti," I told Joe West again.

"I will," he said.

What I got was a title elimination fight with another top five fighter: Luis Manuel Rodriguez, the former welterweight champion who was managed by Angelo Dundee. I lost a split decision. That depressed me terribly. Not just because I had lost, but because I beat myself by being careful and not "freewheelin' " like Joe had always encouraged me.

"Don't worry about it," Joe West said, consoling me after Rodriguez. "We gotta lotta things inna fire yet. Yer still top ten in the world."

My next fight was in Canada. I was supposed to fight a Jimmy Carter there, but he backed out at the last minute. The promoters wanted to replace him with my sparring partner. "It wouldn't be much of a fight," I said.

Joe West agreed. "Hell, they work out with each other every day. They know each other's act."

"Bring him up," the promoter said. "It'll be a good payday for him."

But when he came up, strange things began happening. The promoter decided to change his name. When Joe West heard about that, he hit the ceiling. "It's not gonna happen," he said. "Ain't gonna be no name changes."

I was told by the promoters to give the fans a good show. "You know, carry him a while, cut him up," they said. I nodded, wondering what was going on.

That's when I went to my sparring partner's room and told him what these guys were trying to make me do. I invited him back to my room to talk. I told him that I didn't want to "cut him up," or carry him. I said I was going to knock him out if I could. He had enough pride to think that I couldn't do it, so he told me to go ahead and try.

"But I like you," I said. "I just don't want to have to do that."

"What are you going to do then?"

"Well," I said. "Why don't you just fall. You know I can beat you, right?" He agreed with that. "Then there's no sense in getting cut up for these clowns for a couple of hundred bucks." He nodded again, thinking it was logical.

That's when I proceeded to show him how we could construct the fight to make it look good. We practiced a few minutes in my hotel room, and then he left. He looked visibly shaken. That's when it hit me, too. "What the hell am I doing?" I asked myself. I didn't have an answer.

Just before the bell that night, after the introduction of my opponent came with the name change, I looked at Joe West. "They changed his name. You said it wasn't going to happen."

He looked mad. "Don't worry, I'll call the papers myself, tell 'em his real name. Jus' be careful out there, an' go easy." I didn't bother to tell Joe West about my deal.

I didn't really know if we had a deal. When I walked out of the corner for the first round, he attacked me like he hated me, hitting me with some good punches. I guess it's a real fight, I said to myself, and prepared for one.

The minute's rest found Joe West berating me for taking it so easy. "Go on out there an' take care a business. We have a fight in Paris comin' an' yah can't be fuckin' around."

I did, and caught him coming at me with a good solid right hand. When he fell, he fell forward. I wanted to pick him up, and ask him if he was faking it. I didn't think he was, but when I finally had the chance to ask about it, he just muttered something and wouldn't answer. Regardless, I felt ashamed of myself for having to hit someone I liked so hard. And ashamed that I would get myself involved with as seedy a deal as these promoters had cooked up. The long slide had begun.

16

Paris

PARIS. City of Light. I hoped it would be. Joe had arranged
for me to fight the top French middleweight, Nessim Cohen.
As our cab neared the outskirts of the city, Joe said, "This'll
be a good fight for you."

"Thistle?" I said, mugging at him.

Joe didn't smile. "Knock off the jokes, Society. You win
this fight and you got a title fight coming."

I didn't know whether I believed him any more. The
Benvenuti loss had been disheartening. To lose so lackadaisi-
cally to Luis Rodriguez had been devastating. Knocking out
my sparring partner as he fought under an assumed name
seemed to be the nadir.

We reached the hotel and checked into our rooms. "I'm
going to take a walk," I said to Joe, "want to come?" I half-
hoped he would. I missed the fun of our early days together.
Freewheeling, footloose, that was us. And now we were in
Paris trying to protect one rapidly dwindling reputation.

"No, you go on. And try to find a place to run. You got to
start tomorrow." His voice was weary. I told myself it was
just jet lag. The thought I wouldn't allow myself to think
was that we had gone one too many rounds together.

I asked the desk clerk if there was a place to run near the hotel. He gave me a quizzical look. In fractured French I explained to him that I was a fighter in training. He seemed to understand. In equally fractured English, he directed me to the Jardin Des Tuilleries, a couple of blocks away.

It was a huge park, symmetrically laid out. Fall had come and the leaves were deserting the trees. At one extreme end of the Jardin sat the Louvre. I walked toward it and then crossed over the Seine on a small bridge. I walked beside the Seine for awhile until I came to the Cathedral de Notre Dame. I was but one of many people standing and staring at it, awed by its beauty. It was getting dark by this time and threatening to rain, so I turned around and returned to the hotel.

I met Joe in the lobby and we had dinner together. I was busy telling about what I had seen, in an excited sort of way. He just picked at his food and listened.

"Wanna go t'the gym tomorrow?" he asked.

"Of course."

"Just wonderin'."

"What do you mean?"

"Why yer so relaxed? You weren't this loose in Italy." He leaned back in his chair and held my eyes.

"This is a different place," I answered. "There's a lot of life here."

He smiled and then cut into his thick steak. "Yeah, I like the French cookin' already."

I was up early the next morning and did three miles of uneventful roadwork. That afternoon we were taken to the gym.

Off to the side of the gym was a group of men, watching everything I did. "They're spies for yer opponent," Joe said to me, handing me my gloves. "Give 'em somethin' t'see." He pointed to the peanut-sized bag that dangled from the large platform in the corner of the gym.

I sauntered over to it, aware that everything I did was going to get back to my opponent. When the timing bell struck, I went to work. *Tototah-tototah-tototah-tototah-tototah.* That bag hummed. I circled around it as I banged it, lifting my legs off the floor. All in all it was a ridiculous exercise. I could punch it with my eyes closed. But when it is done smoothly, it can be hypnotic, mesmerizing.

"Good one," Joe West said as the bell sounded. "Let's get back t'the hotel."

I slept poorly the next night. Up at dawn, I went to the park and started running hard. Then a creeping itch began to bother me beneath my sweat suit. I ran to the cover of the trees and pulled up my shirt. A rash of little red bumps covered my stomach.

The city was awake by this time and people were starting to move through the park to get to work. A wispy fog hugged the ground. I sat in the trees and scratched and swore at the rash. The people would see me among the trees and pull up their collars and walk by a little faster. Then a uniformed man approached me cautiously, saying something in rapid French.

"No parley vous Français," I said, still scratching my stomach.

He raised one eyebrow and repeated what he had said before. I took it to mean I better get out of there. I ran back to the hotel, the itch getting worse and worse, and ran to Joe's room.

"What the fuck," he said bending over and looking at the rash on my stomach.

"It came when I ran this morning."

"Looks like a pickle," he said.

"It's killing me, Joe," I said, walking past him to sit on his bed, all the while scratching it.

"Don't sit onna bed!" he said raising his arms to his nightcap. "Don't touch nothin' in here. An' stop that scratchin' . . ." He then walked to the gym bag and after rummaging around in it, threw a tube of cream at me. "What'd you touch?"

"Nothing," I said, rubbing the cream over my stomach and arms.

He held his chin and watched me. "Maybe it's the silk sheets. I'll tell 'em t'change 'em."

"I slept on the blankets last night because it was so hot."

"I wasn't hot," Joe said. "Go back in yer room and shower. See if that helps."

I finished the remains of the tube and tossed it back to him. He jumped out of its way and let it hit the floor. "I ain't touchin' that shit," he said. "Now take a shower an' see what happens. I'll meet you for breakfast inna hour."

I nodded and started to reach for the door handle. He jumped at it and said, "Hold it! I don't wanna have you touchin' nothin' in here."

I then showered, shaved, and made my bed, noticing that the rash had subsided. It made Joe happy when we met for breakfast. "Probably just a quick virus," he assured me.

But that afternoon in the gymnasium it came back. "Jesus, Joe. It just comes when I sweat." He stared wide at it and hustled me out of the room. He didn't want word to get around that his fighter was having any trouble. That's one thing that gives an opponent more confidence than anything —knowing the other guy is having trouble.

At dinner that night, Joe ordered his usual beef steak, and I, my salad and fish. When it was delivered, and I was ready to put my fork into it, he cleared his throat and stopped me.

"Jus' a minute, Society," he said, looking from side to side. "Let's switch plates." He reached quickly and grabbed my plate, sliding his over in front of me.

"What?" I said flabbergasted.

"Poison," he said.

"Poison? Isn't that a little paranoid?" I grinned.

"What'd you call paranoid that's real?"

I shrugged and looked at his steak that was sitting in front of me. "I don't like beef, Joe. I can't eat this." Joe knew I was on a strict health food diet and would often try to con me into eating meat. "Is this some sort of a trick?"

He shook his head. "Man, European fighters'll do anything t'get victory over an American."

"But poison the food?"

"You explain the rash then?" he said, leaving his mouth open and arms spread. "I seen it t'many times what'll happen. They poison you jus' enough t'interrupt yer trainin', mess yer mind."

I shook my head and ate the beef, chewing every bite to the consistency of soup. We ate in silence. I thought about what Joe said. Poison the food?

The next day's roadwork found the rash returning. I just could not work up a good sweat. Joe asked me that morning at breakfast about it and I told him that I hadn't done any roadwork because of it.

"Well, how'd yah sleep last night?" he asked, pouring sugar in his coffee.

"I didn't," I said, propping myself up on the table with my elbows and arms. "I just lay there and scratched the itch."

He looked concerned and thought for a second. "Well, I'll call the promoter an' see if he'll postpone it. If yah can't train, yah can't fight."

"No, don't do that."

"Fight's only a week away. This one's t'important t'be takin' a chance with."

"I'll be okay," I assured him.

But I wasn't. The code is that athletes play hurt. Sick or well, I was working under that macho ethic.

The next few days I began to conceal the rash from Joe. I'd see him every morning after roadwork and say, "Good work, three good ones." He would believe me and start talking about the future we had together.

It was after one of those early runs and long afternoon walks that I returned to the hotel and found Joe West sitting in the lobby, apparently in deep thought. When he saw me walk in he smiled and stood up, motioning me quickly over.

"Where yah been?" he said, letting his grin cross his thin face.

"Went to the Louvre to look at the paintings."

He nodded. I could see that he wanted to tell me something, but that he wanted to build up a suspense. Then he chuckled. "Frequency and probability, man. When yah see a guy enough, yah know he wants somethin'."

"What are you talking about?" I asked.

He faked a punch at my head and bent at the knees, easily tossing one to my body.

"Guess who's in town? And wants to see you . . ."

"Who, man?" I said, without humor.

"Bruno Amaduzzi." Watching the surprise gather on my face, he burst into a cackle.

"What's he want?"

Joe laughed. "You."

"What do you mean, me?"

"He wants to be yer manager," Joe West said simply, as if it were easily understandable.

"What did you tell him?"

"That I had to talk to you. He was a little surprised at that."

"Why would that surprise him?"

"Oh, man," Joe West said, looking away for an instant and bringing it back. "Fighters are traded around here s'often, they don't know who's managin' from day t'day. Around here the managers make the decisions."

"You make the decisions," I said to Joe West.

"Only the ones you want me to make," he said. I told him

I didn't feel like talking about it. All I wanted to do was get some rest before I had to go to the gymnasium.

"Aw'right," Joe said. "But don't do no fuckin' sleepin' up there. That's why you can't sleep at night, yer sleepin' all day!"

When I reached my bed, I thought about Bruno Amaduzzi. That made me remember Nino Benvenuti's last fight on television. He was fighting an unknown fighter from Argentina and having a tough time with him. Then in the twelfth round, a long, paralyzing right hand struck at Nino's chin, shattering it and knocking him out. The unknown was fighting him the way I was until they disqualified me. His name was Carlos Monzon.

"Let's go," I heard Joe West say, rapping on my door.

The gym? I thought. "It can't be that late," I said, opening my eyes.

"I told yah not t'sleep, goddammit."

I rolled over and flicked off the radio. "I wasn't, I was just—"

"Restin' yer eyes, I know," Joe interrupted. "I'll be inna lobby."

I pulled my shoes on and walked downstairs. I had to stop in my tracks. There was Joe West sitting and talking with Bruno Amaduzzi. A small smile crept to my face.

Bruno got to his feet quickly and embraced me.

"Well," Joe said. "We have to go to the gymnasium now." We all shook hands again and Bruno left.

"He really likes you," Joe smiled, getting in the car.

"Yeah. Now what's this crap about him wanting to be my manager? I thought I had one—you."

"He wants t'get yah the fights, have control over yah an' bring yah t'Europe an' make a European fighter outta yah."

"What?" I said in disbelief. The car made a sharp turn and threw me against Joe West. "What would you do then?"

"Oh, I'd still handle yah, but inna figurehead position."

"My trainer then."

Joe shook his head. "No, he wants yah t'work with some a his men on some things." Then he gazed out the car window. "Said yah had some things t'learn."

I felt confused, as if I wasn't getting the whole story. "Then no one would know about Bruno . . ."

"I guess," Joe West said.

Things were clearer now. Joe turned serious and cleared his throat. "He's said we'd split it fifty-fifty."

"What was that again?"

"The money," Joe West said staring at me, as if he were trying to get a reaction out of me.

I thought for a second. "You mean you and I would only get a quarter apiece."

"Like he said, a quarter a somethin' is better than a hunnert percent a nothin'."

I couldn't believe this was for real. "Is this on the level?" I asked.

Joe West hunched his shoulders forward and bobbed his head once. "Funny waya puttin' it, but I think he's serious."

17

The Rash

THE RASH GREW STEADILY WORSE after the Bruno Amaduzzi meeting. Every time I tried to talk to Joe about him, he changed the subject to the rash. I kept trying to change the subject back to Amaduzzi. We kept going around in circles.

At roadwork the next morning I was determined to break the itch. I ran easily to the park and then started sprinting as hard as I could. I refused to let it bother me. I gritted my teeth like a madman, sweating and puffing. The itch was killing me, but I ran a good two miles.

I jogged back to the hotel and walked to my room. I saw Joe's door open as if he were waiting for me. I tried to slip in before he could see the results of the run.

"That you, Society?" he asked. I didn't answer and fumbled with my key, stabbing at the lock. "Aw'right," Joe West said, peeking out his door. "If yah tryin' t'hide it, then it can't be no better. This fight is off."

"No, no," I said quickly. "It's getting better every day."

He walked toward me, grumbling. "If it went away now, it wouldn't make no difference. Yah ain't been able t'train since yah been here. The damn fight's only a couple days away. An' I know yah ain't been gettin' no sleep. I hear that fuckin' radio a yers all night."

"Well, call a doctor then," I said. "I'm telling you it's alright."

He stared at me and thought it over. "Okay, but we'll jus' see what they say. I'll call the promoter an' see if he has one."

Later that afternoon our driver took us to a suburban doctor the promoter had recommended. He looked at the rash casually and handed me some hand cream.

"That shows yah how smart I am," Joe winked. "That's like the stuff I gave yah."

I found it hard to believe. "Hand cream!" I said back in the car on our way back to the city. "Twenty years of education and he gives me hand cream."

"Hands, stomach, what's the diff?" Joe said.

That afternoon in the workout the rash got worse. But now I was keeping it completely to myself. Joe was set to cancel the fight if it bothered me the least bit.

"How yah feel?" he asked me, handing me a towel after the workout.

"Really good," I said, breathing hard, refusing the urge to scratch my stomach. He led me to the dressing room and I waited until he was gone before undressing. I didn't want him to see it.

Joe West returned to find me already dressed. "Yah worked good today. Did yah see yer critic watchin' yah, an' when yah hit that fighter with that left hook?"

I smiled, too, savoring the moment. It came in the sparring just completed. I hadn't been looking very sharp in the gym all week because of my lack of sleep and the itch. I saw the critic standing on the ring apron so I maneuvered my sparring partner over to him and faked a left jab at his head. Then I remembered Joe West's instructions, "Fake a jab, uppercut, an' hook."

The sparring partner went for the fake and ducked into the uppercut. It straightened his head up and I let fly with a hard left hook. It caught him on the side of his head and he sagged to his knees.

"Take it easy in there, now," Joe advised, smiling at me.

At dinner that night I was tired and beat from the hard day's work. I merely picked at the steak Joe West had shoved in front of me. He insisted on our changing plates at every meal. I felt weak and irritable.

"If they were poisoning the food, then you'd also have the rash," I said testily when Joe West slid the plate over.

"If it only comes when yah sweat, how would I get it?"

"Maybe that's the problem here," I shot back. "You don't do any sweating."

I got up from the table quickly and went to my room. I was steaming, so I picked up a book to read and sat in a small chair by the window. Joe came up shortly after and apologized.

"That's okay," I said. "I'm just a little jumpy. I don't like you talking about canceling the fight and stuff. I came here for a fight and all this shit about poisoning the food is getting to me." I shook my head and set the book aside. "I just want to fight and that's all, okay?"

Joe nodded. "Well, I wanna see that rash tomorrow after yah run, aw'right?"

I waved him out of the room. I was really tired from this kind of thing. All I wanted to do was fight. Joe had said a long time ago that it was my career and my decisions. There was no way I was going to pull out of the fight.

The next morning I dressed in my gear and walked outside. Instead of running to the park, I walked. Instead of working hard, I sat on the front steps of a perfume shop facing the Louvre. Then I walked back to the hotel and tiptoed to my room so Joe wouldn't hear me in the hall.

I walked quickly to my bathroom sink, ran some hot water,

and then dumped half a dozen salt tablets into it. Then I splashed my face and sweat clothes with the solution and went to Joe's room.

"Man, you really musta ran this mornin'," he said feeling the water on the sweat shirt. "Let's see the stomach."

I pulled the shirt up. No rash, nothing. He brushed his hand across it and put his fingers to his lips. "Mmmm," he said smackin' them. "I can tell when a prizefighter's ready. They taste it."

"Yeah," I answered.

I asked him if he had heard any more from Amaduzzi, and he just shook his head. "Later."

But later that afternoon after a hard workout, Joe saw that the rash was indeed still there. "Aw'right. No more bullshit, yer goin' home."

"It's going away," I complained.

"You said it was gone. I'm callin' the promoter. This fight is off."

After saying that he stormed off to a telephone and called the promoter. He returned a few minutes later. I was through with my shower and completely dressed, ready for the ride back to the hotel. He had his hands in his pockets, his head bowed.

"What did the promoter say?" I asked.

He tilted his head to the side and shrugged. "That he has a full house, an' it's too late t'find a replacement for you." Then he opened his eyes wider and cocked his head. "Now tell me, how do you really feel?"

I saw my chance and knew I had him. "Great, Joe. I really feel great. You saw me this morning; no rash, and that was after a good hard work!"

"You know everyone around here wants t'see the American and Frenchman . . ."

"Well let's fight then," I said.

"We'll see how it is tomorrow, man."

Tomorrow didn't matter to me, I knew I was going to fight now. Joe wouldn't pull me out of a fight with only a couple of days' notice to the promoter. I was foolishly happy that I could have "tricked" him.

After my roadwork the next morning, the rash was still there. Before I could sneak into my room and hide from Joe West, he came out of his room and spied me.

"Jus' get done?"

I looked up. "Yep."

"Well, let's see yah now." He walked over and lifted my sweat shirt. "Man, it's still there—plain as day . . ."

I knocked his hand off of my shirt and said, "Joe, it's getting better. It doesn't bother me any more. I'm going to fight this guy . . ."

"But yah ain't done no trainin' here t'speak of, or sleepin' for that matter. Yer weak, man!"

I shrugged. "Just call the promoter then, see if he can get us to another doctor. If he stops me from fighting, then I won't fight."

Joe West hesitated, fighting his better judgment, and nodded. "Okay, we'll see one more doctor, and leave it up to him."

That night a car met us at the hotel and drove us to a second doctor. Joe and I stood in his cluttered office, amid pictures of his family and stacks and stacks of manila envelopes and medical journals. His examining table and the other equipment in the office looked like nineteenth-century relics.

The doctor was old and wizened but pleasant. He listened to a rambling explanation I gave of my trouble. He ran his hand over the visible redness on my stomach.

Then he walked directly to a large brown cabinet and removed a bottle of pills. He took a solution off another shelf and removed a needle from a drawer. He handed them to me and then he gave us his instructions.

"Gimme the pills and that other thing," Joe West said in the car. Then he broke out in a chuckle. "Imagine them givin' yah pills jus' before a fight. An' that other thing! A needle to give yerself a shot?"

I said, "No, let me keep them."

"I know yer not gonna use 'em."

"Course not. I just want to see what the stuff is. I'm going to take it home and let my doctor see what they were going to give me."

Joe agreed. "Yeah, that's what I was gonna do."

I began to itch that night again. The room seemed to be a hothouse, causing me to sweat. I couldn't sleep at all. I tossed and turned ceaselessly. Then I remembered the pills and the needle.

I quickly got out of bed and walked to my coat, grabbing the stuff out of the pocket. I tried to remember the instructions. I immediately gulped down four pills. I picked up the needle kit. I prepared everything on my bed and I lifted the needle up. I felt like a desperate junkie.

"What the fuck am I doing?" I muttered, turning around and tossing it into the metal wastebasket. It rang clear, hitting the side of it and plopped to the bottom.

I crawled into bed again and finally fell into a deep sleep until Joe woke me up the next morning. It was my first real sleep in a week, and though I felt like running hard I didn't. I simply walked for a long time. I showed Joe there was no rash.

"I feel like fighting this son of a bitch, Joe," I said.

He smiled at me and winked. "Society Red, yer gonna."

18

Nessim Cohen

"Is Bruno going to be there tonight?" I asked Joe. He nodded as he checked all of our gear bags, making sure nothing was forgotten or misplaced. The driver started the car and Joe told him to take us to the Palleis dello Sports, the boxing arena.

"Well, what do you think about all this?" I asked Joe again. I had been trying to corner him for a week about Bruno Amaduzzi.

"He's throwin' a party for you tonight at the hotel," Joe West answered, evading the key question.

"He made a hell of an offer," I said to Joe, getting to the meat of the subject.

"Yeah, what do you think about it?" he asked.

"If that's the way everyone does it, O.K. by me," I said.

"Does what?"

"Gets the championship, or to it."

Joe frowned. "Not everyone does it like that. I don't know what his deal really is anyway. First he wanted you to come to Italy an' work with his men on some things, and then he wants all the money. I don't really know where I fit into his whole deal."

"Well, what do you think about it?" I asked again, force-fully.

Joe West lit a cigarette and inhaled it deeply. "Well," he said carefully. "These deals aw'ways work both ways. If they wanna make you a European fighter, then you'll have to go along with 'em. But you might be gettin' yerself trapped."

"But if he could get us another title fight . . ."

"With whom? Benvenuti ain't the champ no longer. Monzon is."

"But Bruno sounded like Nino would win it back. Besides, he probably owns a piece of Monzon anyway and couldn't care less either way."

"Could be," Joe West shrugged, staring out the window again.

"Well, tell me what to do?" I finally asked.

He casually tapped the ashes off the end of his cigarette and looked into my face. "I wouldn't touch it with a ten-foot pole. These kinda deals are shit. What the hell is a silent manager? There's too much a that shit goin' on now as it is without addin' to it."

"Then you wouldn't do it?"

"I told you no."

"Well, why are we talking with them?"

He grinned and ruefully added, "You aw'ways wanna be polite t'people. If people wanna talk, you aw'ways wanna listen. Just aw'ways remember that they're talkin' t'you because you got somethin' they want."

I sat back in the seat and tried to drive the topic from my mind. It was too attractive an offer, however, to totally ignore and I actually looked forward to the party after the fight. I couldn't get away from the fact that I really liked Bruno Amaduzzi.

"The party's at the hotel, huh?" I asked.

"Yeah, and Mrs. Scaravel'll be there, too," Joe West answered, with gleaming eyes.

"The lady lawyer?"

Joe West nodded as the driver stopped in front of the arena. "Grab one a the bags there, Society. Let's get t'work."

I was sharing a dressing room that evening with a black lightweight from New York. After he went down the long corridor, through the aisles to the ring, I was alone. I got dressed and then waited for Joe to come back and wrap my hands. In a few minutes, the black lightweight came back into the room with his handlers. He had a large bleeding cut over his right eye. They had stopped the fight.

Joe had been upstairs watching him. "They robbed him. It was like Italy all over again. They wouldn't let 'em fight. He was winnin' it too."

"You mean no ducking?"

"You can duck here," Joe West remarked. "If it's into a punch." Then he smiled at his own joke. "Now get up and get loose, I want you ready for this guy when that bell rings."

"Can you coach from the corner?" I asked, snapping my arms out in front of me and pulling them back like I was rowing a boat.

"I dunno. We'll see what happens. Sometimes I can get away with it, an' sometimes I can't." Then he raised his eyes. "You shouldn't need me hollerin' at you anyway. You should have it in here." He winked and tapped his forehead.

"I do. I just like it replaced fresh now and then."

He grinned and jerked his head around. "C'mon, get loose."

Then they called for us. I gathered my wits together. Joe helped me put my robe on. But there was no excitement to the announcement as there had been in previous fights. Usually when they called my name, my stomach became weightless and turned over and over—until that first punch. But this time I had no reaction. I was a little bored by the whole proceeding.

The din of the crowd enveloped me as I walked up the aisle to the ring. The overhanging balconies were so close I felt I could reach right up and shake someone's hand. Surrounding the arena were bright red and yellow signs advertising gasoline and tires, exactly like the signs one sees in Grand Prix racing.

The crowd welcomed me politely as I stepped into the ring, and cheered when I did my shadowboxing jig, firing quick, little punches into the air. Joe leaned on the ropes and watched me.

"Hard or soft?" he grunted, staring at the canvas.

I spun around and stopped, then danced away. Coming back to him I nodded. "Soft."

"Built for a puncher then," Joe West said, realizing that soft rings hinder fleet-footed boxers.

My opponent entered the ring to unrestrained cheering. I glanced at him and he looked serious, even as he bowed gracefully to the crowd. He was about the same height and weight as I, but his receding hairline made his head look like all forehead. Both his flat nose and a pair of scar-laced eyebrows attested to previous vulnerability. It promised to be an interesting night. He was the puncher and looked it. I was the boxer who would stalk him.

"There's Bruno and Mrs. Scaravel," Joe said, pointing them out.

I nodded toward them and they smiled and waved, and then quickly spoke between themselves.

"Now get ready for this guy," Joe warned, listening to the introductions.

"Take care a business," he said, offering his hand. I took it and nodded and waited for the bell. I rocked back on one leg and when it came walked straight toward Cohen. He backed off warily and I slowly pursued him around the ring. I jabbed a few times and caught him in the nose, feeling it squish at the end of my glove.

That prodded him to counter with a hard, reckless right hand. I had heard that he wasn't a fighter of great polish, but he was usually around for the last bell. I ducked his right and the round ended.

"Yah gotta move better 'n that," Joe West said, jumping into the ring. I sat down quickly on the stool and exhaled hard. Joe lifted a tape-covered water bottle to my mouth. "Spit it out," he ordered.

"My legs are tired," I finally said.

"Yer what?! It's the second round comin' . . ."

I shook my head, remembering the sleepless nights and the drugs, and then the lack of training. "I know it."

"Aw'right then. Yer gonna have t'take it t'em easy. Don't make no unnecessary moves out there. An' when yah inna clinch, don't let 'em know yer breathin' hard."

"Right," I said, biting into my mouthpiece.

Joe held my chin for a second and looked deeply into my face. His eyes were almost desperate and he bit his lower lip. The ten-second buzzer chased him from the ring. "Now be careful out there."

I stood up as if nothing was wrong, waiting for the bell. I hoped this feeble show of strength would intimidate Cohen. I started thinking quickly about tactics. If I can bluff this guy for a couple of rounds, I thought, then I'm going to be able to win it.

The next few rounds were even. I still stood up before the bell started each round and tried to look menacing. Every time I got within range of striking Cohen, I feinted and bluffed a punch. Only a man with a reputation could get away with that kind of offense.

I sat down heavily at the end of the fourth. Joe grabbed my mouthpiece and slapped my face gently. "Yah aw'right?"

I nodded that I was.

"Make sure you tell me when the round is half over," I said. I was hurting.

"Here," Joe said. "I got some Vaseline onna back a my hand. I'm gonna wipe it on quickly."

I nodded and glanced across the ring to the Frenchman. His corner men were making excited gestures, urging him to fight. He sat there impassively.

"Here's yer mouthpiece," Joe said. "Stand up an' look tough, an' go after that cut!"

I stood up and stared across the ring at Cohen. I had cut his forehead in the previous round. The blood streamed down his face like a hundred river tributaries. I was going to make that trickle a torrent.

At the bell he looked like a different fighter. He had more confidence and began asserting himself. In the clinches he punched, and as we sparred, he began grunting with a mindless fury. I tried to get to the cut but couldn't.

"Yah gotta move out there," Joe said at the end of the round, grabbing my waistband away from my stomach. I sat down and nodded, breathing hard and fighting to get oxygen deep down in my lungs. I felt like there was someone choking me. I was under water, trying to swim to the surface.

"I'm tired, Joe. Real tired."

"Quit thinkin' that way, goddammit!"

I shook my head and propped it back against the corner of the ropes. I stared at Joe and he reached into his pocket and pulled a little white capsule out. He snapped it in half and it turned a fluorescent red. He held it under my nose and told me to breathe deep.

"What the fuck is it?" I said turning away from it.

"Smellin' salts. Now breathe it, goddammit."

I put my face into it and breathed. Its fumes seared

through my senses and popped my eyes open. "I'm okay, I'm okay . . ."

"Well move, goddammit."

The bell rang and the Frenchman attacked me. I couldn't move out of the way any more. An essential part of my arsenal—my legs—had been taken away. I just couldn't move.

Cohen realized that and began measuring me with a straight left. Then he would come over the top with a right like a carpenter hammering a nail. Every one struck my face or the sides of my head. I tried to fight back, bob and weave, but my legs wouldn't answer the command of my brain. I saw everything coming and could do nothing but cover up.

When the bell rang signaling the end of the round I didn't know where I was. I staggered at center ring for an instant and thought I heard Joe West whistle. I turned to the voice and saw him sliding the stool between the ropes. He waved me over.

Pop-pop-pop went more smelling salts. I breathed deep but couldn't feel anything. Then some invisible wall seemed to collapse and the tart and burning smell came through.

"I'm okay, okay," I said, pushing his hands away slowly, like a drunk in a stupor.

"How yer legs?"

"Better." I breathed thickly, taking a swig of water. Then I looked down to see if I had any. I could feel nothing but a creeping pin-prickling numbness.

"Yeah, what legs," Joe West said. "Yah don't even know if yah have any. I'm stoppin' this fight."

I pushed the bottle away and cursed him. "You do that and I'll never fight again, you bastard."

He looked surprised and returned my mouthpiece. "Okay. But yah better move. Yah can still win this fight."

"Give me my mouthpiece," I demanded.

"It's in yer mouth . . ."

I flashed a look at Joe's eyes and he was almost crying. He knew he shouldn't have let me fight. A manager should know better than to listen to a fighter who is hung up in dreams of always fighting the odds.

"Now move out there," was Joe West's last warning.

I stood up at the bell but knew it was a lost cause. The Frenchman pounced on me as his countrymen urged him to the kill. He kept slamming my body and head with punches —overhand, underhand, sideways. I merely gritted my teeth and tried to fight back.

I was pushed against the ropes, reeling from another over-hand right. My head was turned away from Cohen, imagining that another punch was coming. I glimpsed Joe poised at the foot of the ring. I thought he was going to stop it.

"Don't stop it!" I screamed out, still imagining a thousand towels raining in the ring like gigantic snowflakes. Again, I sounded like a drunk.

Cohen stepped back wide-eyed at my scream. Then I tightened my fists and went after him. I wanted to kill him, to hit him with everything I had, to break his back and tear out his eyes. I heard the *pop-pop-pop* of more smelling salts. All of the colors at ringside jerked past me, allowing my eyes no focus whatsoever.

"Is it over?"

Joe West shook his head dejectedly. "They stopped it. Yah got knocked out."

"Not off my feet?" I couldn't believe it.

Joe West shook his head again. "It woulda been better had yah gone down, that way yah coulda cleared yer head."

Then the Frenchman walked to me and shook my hand and hugged me tightly, whispering tired French into my ears.

"Let's go, Society," Joe West said, holding open the ropes.

We walked back to the dressing room. I stopped at the bathroom first to look at myself. I felt like I didn't have a head any more, my face was a gargoyle mask of cuts and bruises. I found the mirror and gazed close into it.

"Nothing," I said to Joe West, surprised.

I looked at Joe standing behind me. He had his head down and was choking back tears. "I'm sorry, Society. I shouldn't a let yah fight." He tried to look at me but couldn't.

"I'm alright," I said, trying to cheer him up. I pointed at my face. "Look here. Not one scar or cut."

He glanced up for a second and shook his head, wiping away some water that was in his eye. "Yah don't have t'be bleedin' to be hurt."

I stared at him and glanced back to the mirror. "C'mon," he then said. "Let's get outta here."

He took me to the dressing room and I stared at the beaten New York fighter. He returned the stare and I shrugged. He sat alone, quiet, but still proud.

"You win?" he asked me.

I shook my head. "Naw, they robbed me."

He also nodded, looking away, reliving his own fight. "I was winnin' too . . ."

That opened the flood gate for excuses. We talked back and forth about what we both could have done better. Neither of us looked at the other as we spoke. We both knew there would be no changing the evening's results.

"Going to be some party at the hotel," I said to Joe as I dressed.

"C'mon, let's get there."

As I walked out of the arena the people hovered around the exits, seeking one last glimpse of what had been an exciting evening for them. They stared at Joe and me as we walked to the car.

The party wasn't that dull at all. Bruno gently scolded Joe for going through with the fight because of my illness, and then said it really didn't mean anything anyway. Mrs. Scaravel was radiant. She talked breathlessly to me about how much I was going to like Italy when I came there to live. She opened a bottle of wine and handed me the cork, explaining that when I got to Italy, I was to give it to her. That meant we would be friends for all time. The cork signified a common bond. I was touched.

"Gimme the cork," Joe West chuckled, leaning over and whispering in my ear. Apparently he knew what to do with such a relationship.

Then Bruno Amaduzzi turned serious. He wanted me in Italy soon to fight with Luis Rodriguez in Rome. I mentioned that he had already beaten me before. Bruno brushed it away easily. "That was in America," he said. He made it sound awfully different in Italy.

When the party broke up, it did with all of us promising to get back together again in Italy. Joe West and I watched Bruno and Mrs. Scaravel move easily into the night. I stood there for a minute with Joe. "There's a lot going on around here that I don't quite understand," I said.

He motioned me upstairs with a twist of his head and nodded. "Don't worry about it. These things always have a way a workin' themselves out. Ain't nothin' gonna happen."

As I walked up the stairs to the room, I felt tired and dizzy. I hoped it was because of the wine, though the amount of punches I had taken earlier in the evening seemed to tell me in a not too subtle way that perhaps my best days were behind me.

"Just get a good rest tonight," Joe West said.

I shut the door behind me. Washed up at twenty-two with nothing ahead of me but dirty old gyms, small paydays, and pain. I even wondered what it would be like to fight some up-and-coming kid.

19

A Walk by the Seine

THE NEXT MORNING I took a walk by the Seine, trying to blot out the horror of the previous evening. By noon I had stopped in a dozen bars and cafes and was thoroughly tanked. I met a thin, floppy-hatted girl in one bar and we talked for awhile, until she invited me up to her place. It was an open flat with a mattress on the floor in one corner between a bookshelf and a wall. We sat on the rug and drank anisette, listening to records.

I glanced at her clock, knowing that I had to get back to the hotel, and then looked at her bed. I stood up.

"Well," I said. "Why don't we take care of business?"

She stared up at me with questioning eyes. I reached in my pocket and felt my money. "C'mon," I said, reaching down and taking her hand, motioning her to the bed.

She stood up with even more puzzlement in her face. That prompted me to pull out my money. "I'll pay for it, don't worry. I know how to take care of business." I felt smug.

She let her hand drop away from mine and flashed daggers at me. "What the fuck do you think I am?"

"A hundred? Two? Three?" I said. "I don't care."

She pushed me and I fell off balance. Just like last night,

I told myself, as I pushed her back angrily. Just fifteen hours ago.

"Get out of here," she said, shaking her head and shuddering. I wanted to hit her and hard. I wanted to tell her that I was a prizefighter.

"What the hell's wrong? I just said let's take care of business."

She opened her door. I walked to it and stood on her porch. She started to close it and I pushed it firmly, holding it open. "Well, what are you?" I asked.

She flashed angry eyes at me again. "What the fuck are you?"

I stared at her and found it hard to answer. A freewheeler, I wanted to say. A raconteur, a bon vivant. All of those. But the words became trapped in my throat.

I thought that she was just another woman. And I was ducking involvement as usual. A prizefighter has to be that way. He pays for the tender and beautiful moments in much the same way he takes a punch, a kind of mechanical give and take. To be the toughest man possible, I had hardened myself against any close relationships. I was purposefully insensitive to sensitive things. A prizefighter has to be a macho stud of lowered consciousness to be successful.

I walked away from her place, still in a daze. I returned to the hotel and lay down, dreaming, wondering, fantasizing. I then fought the fight again and again until I must have just passed out.

After the Paris fight I ran into Mike and Rich again, and became involved in a small, good restaurant that they were starting in Seattle. It gave me a place to hang my hat and talk to people outside the fight game.

I told Joe West I wanted a rest from it for awhile, that I was tired of training, traveling, and all the deals.

"Aw, what deals?" he said. "Yer lookin' at it from a microscope. Nothin' can stand that. What yah gotta do is step back an' get the overall view. That sorta thing isn't that common."

"Well, let's fight at home then," I said. "I'm tired of fighting everybody in their own backyard. Let's get off the defensive and call our own shots."

"It's not that easy," Joe West answered. "There's too much shit an' hassle here in Seattle. I gotta deal with people that don't do many things right."

"I thought I was looking through a microscope?"

Joe West shrugged. "Look, yah can get off the road if yah want for a while, but yer too much of a freewheeler and hustler to stay off it for long. Yer too much like me t'quit somethin' that gives yah that freedom."

"Oh, no," I said, not liking the way that sounded. "I won't be doing this when I'm fifty." As soon as I said it, I was sorry. Joe West lowered his eyes. He never had real cause to think his way of life as foolish before, but his crestfallen face showed that I had just given him cause to.

"Well," he said wearily. "If yah can find what I've found in it, you'll be a happy man."

I did rest for awhile, but consented to fighting Cohen again in Seattle. But I got hurt in training and had to call it off. That led to a tuneup fight in Edmonton, Canada, which I won in the ten-round distance. Then I fought the Frenchman again. But I was still psyched out from our first bout. I kept seeing all of those right hands from our initial encounter. Like the fight against Luis Rodriguez, I became too cautious.

"Freewheel out there," Joe West berated me between rounds. "A prizefighter gotta freewheel."

It didn't work. I lost a split decision to him and I returned to the restaurant to figure things out. I became extremely reflective there. I talked at length to Mike and Rich about all of the deals that I had heard of and how prizefighting wasn't exactly what I had once thought it to be. I would sit around and look at my fists, wondering how the very things that could make love could also bring pain. And I also wondered why I was getting so introspective, knowing only too well that a prizefighter, a real prizefighter, wouldn't be thinking that way. If he examines it philosophically, it just doesn't seem to make much sense. When analyzed closely, it's silly to be beating someone up for money.

20

South Africa

"TACTICS," Joe West said. He looked up from behind his bifocals. "That's what's gettin' us here." Then he began filling out the alien cards heralding our arrival at Jan Smoots Airport, Republic of South Africa. He had spread our passports out in front of him and was busy cross-checking all the facts to make sure everything was right.

"What's this?" I said, picking up one sheet. "This says you're European, not Negro."

"Don't start no shit here. That's the only way they'll let me inna country."

I had never bothered to consider that a black man who was manager of a white prizefighter might not be acceptable in South Africa.

"Well, what are you going to tell them?" I laughed. "That you left your sun lamp on?"

"I said don't be startin' no shit. Everything's fine." He tried to sound stern but I saw the smile begin to curl on his lips.

"This has got to be the coup of the century."

He chuckled and asked, "What's coo mean?"

"A master stroke of tactics and opportunity."

"Well then, there yah go," he nodded quickly. "That's 'zactly what it is."

I then began to read the paper. "It says you're French, and Swedish, and . . ."

"That's right. I'm everything," he added. "Jus' don't start no political things. The last thing we need is an incident."

I couldn't stop from grinning. "Who's going to meet us?"

"The promoter," he said. "He's a polio, can't walk. He should have someone there with 'im, too."

"A paraplegic, huh?" I said.

"I don't know if they're both polios," Joe West shrugged. "Or plegics, or whatever yah call 'em."

We were met by four men, one of whom was being pushed along in a wheelchair by a blank-faced black man with close-cropped hair. The man in the chair had a ruddy complexion and dark, thick eyebrows. He was Maurice Toweel, the fight's promoter.

One of the other men was about my height with an angry-looking scar cutting diagonally across his eyebrow into the top of his nose. He was my opponent, Pierre Fourie. The third man was his manager. They introduced themselves and then left.

"Did yah see that cut?" Joe West said, as we were driven to our hotel.

"It only looks to be about two weeks old. I could see the stitchmarks still there."

"One good punch, man. Tactics . . ."

Maurice Toweel, also in the car, heard us and nodded. "There are a lot of promoters, or would-be promoters in Jo'burg. The dates for the fights are given far in advance of the day, so we dare not back out of a fight or another promoter will step in and take it."

I didn't get the gist of it and Joe hadn't either, so we looked at each other and raised our eyebrows. Then Joe lowered his voice. "This might be the one, Society. One good punch on that eye and brother, it's yours. Use twistin', sharp punches out there."

I punched out with a small twisting punch and Joe nodded smugly. Maurice Toweel glanced around and saw my twisting punch and Joe West's laughter and watched us closely.

Toweel explained that the fights were well attended here, but that there was a lot of promotion to be done. "You are here two weeks before the fight, so it can be sold," he said. "And it should be a good one. You are the first real world class fighter our Pierre has met."

Joe nodded. "It'll be a good win for us." Then he jabbed me in the ribs.

"One twisting punch," I said on cue. Maurice Toweel still kept his eyes on us.

Our black driver by this time had steadily increased the speed of the car. We were really moving. Joe looked concerned. Toweel noticed his feelings and admonished the driver who promptly slowed down.

"You have to watch them," Maurice explained.

"Yeah," Joe West said dully.

When we arrived at the hotel in the country, Joe West looked at it and shook his head. "Unacceptable. I want my fighter in the city. Fighters gotta be in the city. Hell, I gotta be in the city. I wanna be able t'get around."

Maurice Toweel agreed and asked us to stay one night, to give them time to prepare a spot in the city. Maurice left, still spitting and snarling at his black man.

That seemed odd to me. Maurice Toweel was totally dependent on this "calfer" for everything, yet he never showed even a rudimentary kindness to him, preferring instead to pick and scold and shout, especially when the driver had to lift him out of the car into his wheelchair. Granted, the driver wasn't too gentle with him, bumping his head on the car door jam and literally pouring and dropping him in his chair. But the abuse that spewed forth so constantly from

Maurice's pursed and growling lips would have pushed me to do much more against him. The black man, however, seemed to be enjoying himself, flashing ivory grins at Joe West and myself.

"That man has some words, don't he?" Joe West remarked about Maurice Toweel.

"Yeah, but did you see the black man's eyes when Maurice yelled at him?"

Joe nodded. "He looks to be jus' bidin' his time."

When we got temporarily settled in the hotel, I dressed in my roadwork gear and hit the streets. I passed long lines of black people standing outside of what looked like a factory. They all wore ragged clothing and headbands of white cloth like those I had seen in history books on stories about the Old South. They watched me silently, as I ran past them.

Returning to the hotel, I saw Joe getting ready for bed. He pulled the bedspread back and slipped between the sheets. He looked up when he saw me. "Better get t'bed yerself."

I said I was coming. I was tired from the flight that had taken twenty-two hours.

"One good, twistin' punch," Joe West said.

"Got'cha," I said. I had a chance.

21

Black on Black

EARLY THE NEXT DAY we were driven into Johannesburg.

"Quite a place," Joe West said as we rode through the downtown area.

I nodded. It was a study in contrasts. There was a hard core, older section of the city that was surrounded by newer, more modern buildings that spread up and out. People walking the streets seemed either well to do or poor, upper class, or lower class, black or white. I saw no happy mediums in South Africa.

"Lookit there," Joe West said, pointing to a couple of park benches. Some had been set aside for whites, others for blacks.

Everyone is exceedingly polite. But the smothering pall that hangs over the city is that smog of apartheid. A hard place to feel comfortable in.

"They say they got us the same suite that Rocky Marciano stayed in," Joe West said. "I told 'em that's good. That we're used t'bein' treated like champs."

The driver stopped at a large hotel on a hill overlooking the downtown area, and three black men dressed in neatly tailored red suits picked up our bags. They carried the bags up to our suite—two bedrooms, a parlor, and a bathroom. Joe gave each of them a silver dollar.

"Thanks bossz," they said. Joe West looked sideways at them.

There were large windows and balconies in each room, and Joe immediately began checking things out. He slid open the door and stepped out. Looking across the street at some construction, he hollered "Look at that, will yah. They don't use no steel in these high risers."

"There's steel in there," I said. "Look at the center of the concrete beams."

"That's pig iron, man. I'm talkin' about steel. A buildin's like a prizefighter, it's gotta have steel in it for support."

"That's why I had t'get outta Los Angeles," he continued. "They done sucked up all the oil outta the earth, just like they done here with their diamond mines. This place might collapse."

"Don't worry about it, Joe," I said. "I have enough steel in me for both of us."

"I kinda figured you did," he said, rubbing his chin.

Once settled in the hotel, Joe West and I began establishing a pattern of movement so we could get comfortable and used to the surroundings. In the mornings, I would usually get up before Joe and be met by the black driver with the angry eyes—Toweel's companion. He would drive me out to the country for two or three miles of roadwork. He was a silent, brooding type of a man, often friendly and often bitter about things. His voice was high-pitched and had traces of a colonial accent. When he understood that he didn't have to call me boss, we became friends.

After my roadwork I'd return to the hotel and wake Joe up. He'd crawl out of bed without saying a word, go to the phone, order coffee, and then sit silently smoking a cigarette until it came. You didn't dare talk until he had that coffee.

"Them eyes," Joe West would say as he sipped at the coffee. "Batter them eyes."

The obeisance of the black room service attendants bothered Joe. One day after I'd ordered some scrambled eggs, one of them said to me, "Okay, bossz," as he set them in front of me.

"He ain't yer boss," Joe West snapped.

The servant looked at Joe and smiled again. "Yes bossz . . ."

"And I ain't either," he added. "Goddammit, be yer own boss. The sooner yah find it out the better you'll be."

I smiled at the whole scene, remembering Joe West's words on the plane. "Don't be starting any shit," I said. "We don't need any incidents."

"Well, crap . . ." Joe West said, shaking his head. "These fuckers look like organ grinder monkeys in them suits." That visibly disturbed Joe. He received more than he bargained for when he decided to "sneak" into the country.

As I ate breakfast, Joe West would usually be pouring over Fourie's record in the *Ring Record Book,* comparing our common opponents. Sometimes he would ask me leading questions about some of Fourie's fights that were supposed to give me more of an insight on how to fight him.

"Aw'right, Society," Joe would say. "Fourie fought this guy awhile ago. He wasn't a very tall fighter, and not much of a puncher. He'd usually work in close, but not consistently. He never seemed to be in top shape. How do you think he did against Fourie?"

"Tell me a little more. How old is he?"

"About thirty."

"Fourie beat him, ten-round decision."

"Right," Joe West would say, laying the book down. "Yah know why? Because the other fella tried t'box 'em. The way yah beat Fourie is t'fight 'em!"

We did a lot of hyping the fight, usually each day after breakfast. Newspapers and radio interviews were the norm. But one day we were told to go to Maurice Toweel's office for an old-fashioned newsreel.

South Africa didn't have television in 1971, so all the big news events were covered by newsreel, which were then shown in the theaters. Fourie and his manager were also in Toweel's office. We were going to stage the contract signing.

Maurice sat at his desk in his wheelchair facing the large cameras on tripods as nervous technicians rushed around trying to get everything right. As they were filming, they told us we could talk about anything we wanted since the sound track would later be dubbed by an announcer. I wanted to do something different, but Joe shook his head and discouraged me. "Just play the game, man," he said. "It's their show."

It was in the late afternoons that Joe and I would just walk around the city, enjoying the sights.

As we walked, Joe trained his eyes on the ground and kicked at small pebbles, many times bending over when something caught his eye. I finally asked him what he was doing.

"Lookin' for diamonds," he said. "This is the diamond capital of the world."

"Get serious," I'd laugh.

"Lotta gold, too," he'd answer seriously, still kicking at the ground. "All yah need is one strike."

Joe also liked the idea that he was passing himself off as a European instead of a black. He would like to enter every shop, browse around, and buy a diamond pinky ring. "Yah wanna get somethin' in every place yah go," he'd advise me. "That way yah can remember where yah been. An' yah can always turn rings in at the hock shop."

"I have enough memories," I'd answer.

He would also like to sit on white-only benches. Every

time he did, he would look at me and laugh that cackle, his joke on the South Africans. When we actually stopped to talk to some Bantus, Joe West would tell them that he was as black as they were. Astounded, they wanted to know everything about the United States.

"Oh, it's gettin' pretty good there," he'd say, putting his arm around me. "Black, white, they're all gettin' along better." A real bona fide ambassador of good will, that Joe West. But he'd always tell the men they were entitled to everything, too, and that they didn't have to stand for what was going on in their own country. "Yah gotta do what yah think's right," he'd say. "And I know yah don't think this is right."

While we were in the city, Joe West and I made good friends with Abe Heck. He was a rival promoter of Maurice Toweel. He knew a lot about Fourie and would have liked nothing better than for me to kick his ass.

We'd meet him for dinner sometimes at his home, and Abe would always have a projector set up in his study to show fight films. When the action got heavy, he would stop the film, replay it once or twice, showing me different punches I could use against Fourie. He also obscurely mentioned that there was a lot of behind-the-scenes stuff in many fights in Johannesburg, and that I should be wary. He didn't elaborate, so I let it pass as the carping of a rival promoter.

At night, after my gym workout, Joe and I would sit at our dinner table in very formal dress, listening to varied radio dramas. During the commercials we'd talk about fighting and the possibilities of my getting another title shot.

"You can get it, man," Joe would say, slicing his steak and chewing the last bite. "You beat this guy an' you got a title fight."

I didn't agree. "Joe, I've lost too many fights in the last two years."

"Only to the big guys," he'd say. "That doesn't hurt. Shit,

they wanna see you with that title. Shit, they was tryin' t'give yah the damn thing. Yer jus' what they need in the middle-weights; fast, colorful, fought the names, an' all that. . . . Man, yer only a kid compared t'every other top contender. They's all thirty or close."

"Maybe," I said, thinking it to be a plausible argument.

After dinner, Joe let me roam by myself around the city. I was determined not to get into any trouble here. I had nothing on my mind but fight.

"Have a beer if yah want," Joe would tell me as I stepped out the door. "It's been hot here an' I don't want yah t'get ready too soon."

There was a nice bar a few blocks from the hotel, and I would usually go to it and try to stir up some conversation about the fight. I usually wasn't disappointed.

"They were always built up to be good fighters," one man told me over his lager. He stared into his drink. "But they didn't ever show me anything. But this Scott is supposed to be a world class fighter, and that might make the difference. Of course, they were always supposed to be able to beat Fourie, but on fight night they seem to lose it."

"What is he?" I asked. "A puncher?"

"No, he's nothing but a boxer, and a pretty fair one at that."

"Who do you think will win then?"

"My money is on Pierre Fourie," he said almost proudly. "He can't be beat here." Then he revised the statement. "Of course, if he gets lacerated, then it's a different story. Pierre was cut badly in his last go, and I think they're going too quick with him now."

I finished my beer and wished him luck on his bet.

Walking back to the hotel, I passed a group of Bantus standing around a fire, talking quickly in their own dialect. The place where they had congregated was in an alley, between two old buildings that were being torn down. Old wood would feed the flames. I decided to stop and try to talk to them. I approached the flickering reflection on the facing building cautiously. When they saw me they became quiet. There were three men, two squatting and one standing up. They eyed me suspiciously.

"Yes?" the man standing said, in a perfect British accent.

"Hello, I'm the prizefighter fighting Pierre Fourie Saturday night," I said walking closer to them.

The man standing translated it to his friends. They didn't look like they bought the story. The translator invited me to sit down. He was a small man, with baggy pants and a black beret pulled back tightly on his head.

"Thanks," I said, pulling a bag of marshmallows from my pocket. "What say we eat these," I said, sticking one on the end of a stick. Seeing that I didn't get any reaction, I smiled. "Pretend that they're the honkys in the government. Come on, we'll burn them!"

The squatting black men looked at the one standing for a translation. He grinned and spoke to them quickly. I don't know if they understood the word honky, but they started laughing uproariously. We passed the sack around until they were gone.

"Do you know anything about Pierre Fourie?" the man in the beret asked me.

"He's a boxer," I said.

Then he proceeded to tell me everything he knew, although he said it was also secondhand information. I asked him why he never had seen Fourie fight. He grinned and slowly shook his head.

"Bantus are not allowed to go to white boxing matches. Bantus have their own boxing matches against other Bantus. They have them in the afternoon," he explained, "because they don't want us out at night."

"Oh? There's a curfew?"

"Yes. It's getting close to it now."

Then I remarked that he spoke very good English. He thanked me and told me that he worked for a man who had taught him, but he had finally decided to run away. "I didn't like him calling me Pepe," he said sarcastically. "For that's what he also called his dog."

"Then you're on the run . . ." I said excitedly. "What if they catch you?"

He glanced over to the right and listened for something that I couldn't hear. He became tense, and then looked me in the eyes. "Have you ever seen that prison over there?" I said I had heard about it. He kept staring at me. "That's where I would go. I hear screams at night from there from old friends."

I nodded, wishing that I could do something for him. He then offered his hand, and I gave him a soul-brother shake. "They do that in America," I said. "It means brotherhood."

He nodded and turned to his brothers, speaking rapidly. They all rose and shook my hand and left into the streets, hurrying to somewhere they wouldn't be noticed.

I stood there for a moment as they scurried away. I had been all around the world with a black man. He was able to get along inside the domain fairly comfortably. Maybe it was his "tactics" or intelligence, I didn't know. But the sight of these men "on the run" made it all come home. It didn't seem right that Joe West could travel around freely because he was with a white prizefighter, an invited guest to every country of his choosing.

I began to feel not only like a meal ticket, but a passport as well.

"I'll be yer best friend in these fights," Joe had often told me. I then began to think that it was the other way around.

22

The Deal

"HAVE THEY TRIED to buy you yet?"

I looked at my sparring partner and had to make sure I was hearing correctly. "What?" I asked.

"Have they tried to buy you yet?" he said a second time.

"Who's they?"

"Well, have they? I know they have to. You are too fast for him."

I stared at him for a second. "Wait a minute," I said, pulling him over to the side of the dressing room, away from the scales where I had been checking my weight. "Now what's this shit about buying?"

"The fighters that come here are usually bought. They look tough and then they get bought. It happens all the time. Most of the people around here know it." He then shrugged and walked away.

I glanced quickly to the gymnasium floor where Joe West was talking to the many people who had come to watch my workout. I had looked good and fast and felt strong. This was to be my last day of sparring and I was happy that it had been a good one.

But my sparring partner's words set off thoughts about Canada and Paris, and even Italy.

That night I brought it up over dinner.

"Hey Joe, what have you heard about fixes here?"

"What?"

"Fight fixes. What have you heard about fight fixes?"

He shrugged. "Not much, the usual. One guy accusin' another."

"You don't think it's true then."

"Naw . . ."

I nodded slowly, chewing my food. "Well, who have you heard it from then?"

"What?"

"The rumors."

Joe West shrugged. "Reporters, people inna gym. It's hard t'put my finger on." He lifted a coffee cup to his mouth and sipped it. Putting it back down, he squinted. "Why? What have you heard?"

I was about to answer when the phone rang. Joe got up to answer it. "Hello," he said. "Hello? Hello? Hello?" Then he smashed it down, muttering, "Somebody's been fuckin' with our phone for the last three or four nights. Every time I pick it up, there's no answer."

He took his seat again across from me and took another sip of coffee. The radio show was just over and more commercials were playing. "Now what have you heard?" Joe West asked.

"That it happens all the time."

"Who told you that," Joe West scoffed.

"That light-heavy I worked with today."

That seemed to make it all right, and Joe West laughed. "Yeah, but he's nuts. You saw how he drove that foreign sports car."

I laughed, remembering the ride home we got from him

one night. It was a wild one, through the streets and sometimes the sidewalks.

"But just the same . . ." I said.

"No just the same about it. This might be what they tryin'
t'do about messin' with yah mind, get yah thinkin' about
somethin' but the fight. Remember, they want this win bad."

I nodded, feeling better. "Yeah, it sounds a little melo-
dramatic anyway."

"You gonna dry out for this one?" Joe said, changing the
subject.

"Yeah. I want to be as light as I can. I want to outspeed
him."

"An' when yer light like that, yer punches is sharper and
cut people up. Twist them punches inna eye, break open
that scar!" Joe exclaimed.

The last two days would be dry days as far as liquid is
concerned. I would want every extra ounce of water out of
my body, so I would look lean and my muscles would have
definition. "I want yah so hard I can strike a match on yer
body," Joe would say.

The night before the fight, Joe West told me that he was
going to see the newsreel that we had filmed at Maurice's
office. I had seen it earlier in the week and told him it was
great. Joe should have gotten an Academy Award.

"I'm right there on the screen, huh?" he'd smile.

"Fifteen feet high."

"Wanna see it again?"

"No," I said. "It's with a lousy Richard Burton film. You
go ahead though."

He wiped his mouth with his handkerchief and nodded.
"I'm gonna then. Be back inna couple a hours."

I picked up a poetry magazine and watched him leave and
then started reading. I used to think it was odd that a prizefighter would take refuge in something like poetry. But it

became a good escape for me from mental and physical rigors of trying to beat somebody up.

A prizefighter before a fight is like a nervous bride. He wants the event to happen, but he can do without the worrying that accompanies it.

The telephone rang. I walked over to it and picked it up. "Hello?"

A voice on the other end quickly whispered to someone standing nearby and it was muffled. Then a strong voice came over it and asked where Joe West was. I thought they might be fans wanting tickets.

"He'll be back in a couple of hours," I said. "Call then, huh?"

They said they would, and I hung up the phone.

Not more than twenty minutes later I heard a knock on my door. I opened it and said, "Yes?" There were two men standing there.

"May we come in?"

"Well, I'm reading now."

"It will only take a moment," the shorter of the two said. He looked up to me with a raised eyebrow and puffed cheeks. His little round eyes were partly hooded with loose skin. I stepped back and let them in.

"I don't know where the tickets are," I said, recognizing the voice of the smaller man as the phone caller.

"That's not what we're here about," answered his friend. He had a bright red shirt on underneath a dark-checked sportscoat. He positioned himself behind the couch the other one sat on.

"What do you want then?" I asked, holding my book of poems.

The man behind the couch looked at me. A beaten nose stuck out between clear eyes. He had no chin. "You're not going to win the fight tomorrow," he said sharply.

I became instantly chilled, remembering my sparring partner's words. "Oh?"

He kept his eyes on mine and stuck a toothpick in his mouth. "Even if you do, you won't get the decision. Follow?"

The man on the couch added, "Pierre has a very good record in Jo'burg. He's coming to title fight and it's going to mean big money. He simply can't afford to lose."

"Oh, you're going to tell him to tear my head off while I'm just letting him hit me, huh?" I said sarcastically.

"Pierre doesn't even know. He's a nice kid with a family."

"Alright, alright," I said shaking my head. "Enough's enough. Just get out of here."

"What are you making for this fight? Five thousand?" the man in the red shirt asked.

His friend on the couch was apparently cued. "If you get knocked out, say in one of the later rounds, showing that Pierre can punch, then we can get four-to-one . . . five-to-one . . . even six-to-one odds. We'll bet money for you. How's thirty thousand sound?"

"You might as well," the man behind the couch piped in. "You aren't going to win anyway. Make it easy on yourself." Then he stepped from behind the couch and showed me how it could be done. "Like this," he said. He played both fighters and then worked himself into a corner and slapped his right cheek and wobbled his knees. "Simple."

I watched and couldn't believe it. My mind flashed to Canada where I was doing almost the same thing. And when the guy buckled his knees, the parallel was complete. I thought hard. What the hell is going on here? I have to tell Joe. Then I pointed to the door. "Both of you better get out. Joe West will be back in a minute, and I don't think he'd enjoy this as much as me."

They glanced at their watches and looked at each other. "Thirty thousand is a lot of money," the man on the couch said, getting to his feet.

I pointed to the door. "And very impossible."

The larger one then walked to me and opened the door, brushing against me. "We'll give you three thousand dollars then to stay away from the cut. Got that? Three thousand dollars to stay away from the eye."

"A little worried, huh?" I smiled, enjoying the feeling that I was getting from two very anxious men who thought I was a good enough fighter to have to be bought so their man could win.

The shorter one then shrugged as if it were not big deal. "You are not going to win anyway," he said casually. "We thought you were a smart fighter, that is what we heard. Maybe we were mistaken . . . ?"

Then we all heard a rustling in the hall. "Good," I said. "It sounds like Joe West. Talk to him if you want."

They exchanged quick glances and checked their watches again. "I'll be at the weigh-in tomorrow," the taller one said, bristling at the neck and still fidgeting with his toothpick.

I raised my head and smiled wider. This was great fun, I thought to myself. "Well, bring a certified check then," I said. "With your name on it."

The smaller man shot a look at his friend and squinted hard, and motioned him out. As he left, he brushed into me and bumped my head on the door. "Tomorrow," he said, raising a finger to my face.

I watched them walk down the hall to the elevators. They were messing with my mind, I told myself. Joe West had told me many times that they try to mess with a prizefighter's mind.

"Bring a check!" I shouted down the hall, then closing the door and laughing, feeling happy that I wasn't letting my mind be messed with. "Messin' with my mind," I said to myself, like Joe West would say it. "No way."

Shortly after they left, Joe West returned in an ebullient mood, apparently from seeing himself made into a movie star via the newsreel. I must have looked a little strange to him, sitting quietly hunched down into the chair facing out the window.

"You know," he said, beginning to chuckle, "I had me a fighter once that I took cross-country for a fight, he could fight, too, but yah know what he did jus' before we went t'the ring? He turned t'me and said he didn't want t'fight this fella! Can yah imagine that? We're about ready t'fight an' he tells me."

I nodded, still thinking about my night visitors. I felt I should mention the whole thing to Joe, but then I thought that he might try and pull me out of the fight like he did in Paris. I didn't want that.

Besides, Joe was getting on my nerves. I felt myself more manipulated than ever. Joe was always doing a number on me. Even in the story he just told me, he had said he took the fighter cross-country. No way! It was the fighter that had taken Joe.

"C'mon," Joe West said, standing in the middle of the room. "I'll show yah what yah gotta do." He motioned me out of my seat and held his hands up. He came in close and noticed my reluctance to put my hands up. "C'mon, see how yah gotta do it."

I grimaced and raised my hands. Joe West then glided across the carpet and twisted a few punches across the distance between us onto my eye. "Like that," he said. "Yah jab an' then cross fast with yer right."

I said, "You remember what I told you my sparring partner said? About those fixed fights?"

"Get that shit outta yer head now," Joe West said sternly, scowling. "People inna fight game talk about it t'mess a man's mind."

"Yeah, but he—"

"He ain't nothin'," Joe West shot back. "Now stick yer hands up there an' I'll show yah what t'do."

I shrugged and raised my hands, watching what to do. Joe pretended to be Fourie. I slid across the carpet, twisting punches to his eye.

"That's it," he said, raising a hand and sitting down, ending the round. He fumbled for a cigarette and added, "Yah fight a guy like this that way, yah move on 'em t'the sides, and then come back with twistin' punches."

I threw one more twisting punch into the air. My arm felt like a corkscrew as it cut through the air, pulling me after it as it uncoiled.

"Now yer gettin' it," Joe West grinned.

I said nothing.

23

Tactics

I AWOKE THE MORNING of the weigh-in not wanting to fight, disturbed by a sleepless night that had been punctuated by violent dreams. I was being slaughtered in the ring. Payoffs. Fixed fights. The two men in my room last night. The "stolen" fight against Benvenuti. Paris and pills. The Edmonton fiasco.

Joe West had told me that deals and payoffs were the exception in prizefighting, but all I had ever seen as a prizefighter were such clandestine affairs. Everywhere I had been seemed to push me a little closer to what was happening now. Every promoter I met, with the possible exception of the Los Angeles bunch, had one thing in mind; submerge the basic idea of a fight and make it a promotion with an expectable beginning, middle, and end.

That disturbed me. Every prizefighter lives a one-punch existence. One blow and everything is final. In a pure prizefight, bare instinct triumphs over artificial value. Now, the line between athlete and entertainer was becoming increasingly tenuous. The promotion game was now the thing. A manager would not let his fighter box away from home too often. The judges were sure to be unfriendly. There was too much to lose. I was just a sideshow.

When I first started, they all told me I was promotable because I was white, college-educated, and could think on my feet. They all wanted me because I was going somewhere, because with all those things going for me I would be an ideal champion. That was the first step I took in their game.

The next step was even easier. If a fighter wanted to be world-class, he had to be a puppet, ready to dance for a handful of extremely powerful men who had about as much love for the sport as a pimp does for his whore.

I wanted badly to tell Joe West that I wanted to go home, and quietly get off the treadmill. This wasn't what I wanted. I wanted something honest. But I was having trouble figuring out just what that was. And by now I just didn't trust myself. Joe West had told me that the oldest fix in the world was the mind fix.

But I had seen more than just "mind fixes." I had had outright offers.

"They mighta slickered us here," Joe West said, as we walked into the theater where the weigh-in was being held. He held the contract for the fight in his hand and tapped it with the back of his fingers.

"What do you mean?"

"I don't think this Fourie is a middleweight at all." He handed me the contract. "See that clause that says if he's over the weight, all they gotta do is forfeit a hunnert bucks?"

"Yeah? So what?"

The room starting filling up with preliminary fighters and spectators. I looked up from the paper briefly to see if the two men that talked to me last night were here. I didn't see them.

"Well, that means he can weigh all he wants for what is a middleweight fight," Joe said.

"He's a middleweight," I said. "He's ranked in the top ten."

"That don't mean shit. I'm not gonna let yah fight no light-heavy. With this contract they could weigh two hunnert pounds."

I thought it over and liked what I was hearing. Maybe I wouldn't have to tell Joe I didn't want to fight. "Well, let's wait and see what the weights are," I said.

Joe West was right. My weight was the lightest it had been in a long time, close to 157. My opponent's was closer to 165, way over the middleweight limit of 160. And as I looked at him he appeared to be in excellent shape, not fat or flabby at all.

"Yer not gonna fight this guy!" Joe said out loud to everyone. "Yah ain't givin' up that much weight to some fighter. What do you take me for?"

Everyone looked startled at Joe West, and I did, too.

"You go back t'the hotel," he said to me. "Let me fight this out. If this guy don't get inna sweat box and lose the weight, then this fight's off, yah hear me?"

I nodded and dressed quickly, leaving the theater. I was happy that the fight didn't appear to be coming off. And I hadn't seen the men again.

But just as I rounded the corner to leave the theater, the man with the red shirt bolted out of a corner and handed me something. "Here, take this," he grumbled. I refused and he stuffed it into my coat pocket, and then walked quickly away. I stood there like a fool, feeling the envelope full of money in my pocket. I started for Joe, whose words were ringing from the theater aisles, and then I got scared. My first reaction was to run in and tell him what had happened. I wanted to pull him out of there before anything could go any farther. But then I became nervously greedy. Three thousand dollars was about as much as I was getting paid. And the fight wasn't going to come off anyway, so it was essentially free money.

I listened for another second to Joe's shouting and then quickly walked to the hotel. I felt euphoric that things were finally going my way, and scared that I had acted so criminally. I laughed to myself nervously, as I reached the room and tore at the envelope. A stack of small bills tumbled out and drifted around my feet. "Jesus," I muttered, bending over and quickly stuffing them back in.

I didn't even bother to count the money. I sat at the desk that looked out the window on downtown Johannesburg. I wasn't quite sure of what to do. I was just hoping that the fight wouldn't come off.

"It's not," I said to myself. "Joe said it wouldn't." I relaxed and then heard him enter the room.

"Hey, Society," he grinned, coming into the parlor.

I spun around and said, "Well? . . ."

"The fight's on," he said simply. "I just wanted t'shake 'em up. Always shake 'em up, that way they never know what t'expect." Then he came over and stood by the desk. "How yah feelin'? How'd yah like my act?"

I looked up and shook my head. "I didn't know it was an act." I felt cheated. I just didn't want to fight this guy now. "What about his weight?" I complained.

"Shit," he said sarcastically. "I wouldn't care if he weighed 180. He ain't never been no puncher. That weight on 'em will make it easier for yah t'move around, take advantage."

He spied the money that sat on the top of the desk. "Hey hey, what's this," he said, picking it up. "The New York money? I wondered where yah was keepin' it."

I watched him counting it and didn't say anything. I had told him that after this fight I was going to vacation in

New York. I stared at his face, so happy, so worry-free, and I got madder.

"Yah gonna have some breakfast?" he asked. I shrugged, hoping that I could somehow communicate that I wasn't as happy as he was. Then he said, "That's good weight for you, know that? I ain't seen yah weighin' like that since we first got together." Then he rubbed his hands together and smiled. "That's a good sign."

Why did I feel so totally manipulated by his words now. I didn't used to feel that way. Everything he had ever said to me now sounded selfish. Christ, it was me that was fighting, not him. I would wear the scars tomorrow, not him. I would bear the stigma of defeat, payoffs, and fear. Joe West would feel nothing.

"I hurt every time yah get hit," he'd say. "The fighter that don't use tactics will get beat by 'em. Slice 'n' splice an' take care a business. Shake my hand, an' take . . . care a business . . . frequency and probability." All words of manipulation.

Why did I have so little faith any more in him or myself? How could I fight under these cirmustances? Why don't I just tell him? Why do I find it so hard to talk to him any more?

"C'mon . . . " Joe West said again.

"Okay, okay," I said. "Have them send something up. I don't want to go out of the room."

24

The Loser

THE FIGHT WAS like a bad dream in slow motion. Every time I came close to Fourie's eye, I hesitated. Every time I tried to hit him, I pulled the punch. All I could think of was how much I didn't want to be here, in this ring, with three thousand dollars extra in my pocket, and unable to talk to Joe West about anything any more. The whole affair was as depressing and cowardly a thing as I had done in my life.

To be honest with Joe was impossible. He still had an image of me as the tough guy, a freewheeler, and a good prizefighter. Somehow though, I blamed him for everything.

When I arrived at the arena that night I was lackadaisical, slow-moving, and full of self-deprecating jokes. Unconsciously I was hoping that Joe West would be able to read those signs and try to really talk to me. But he held hard and fast to his conception of me as a tough guy prizefighter.

I just sat in the dressing room and watched the other fighters prepare for their battles. Some were laughing, some making the sign of the cross on their chest, and some were just sitting in the corner like I was, watching everyone else.

I divided the winners and losers up this way. The reflective-looking fighters were the ones who were going to lose. They were still asking themselves the questions of why and what for. Watching them now became like looking in a mirror. After they lost, they walked back to the dressing room without tears or screams that they were robbed, just merely stepped back into their clothes, happy that they had at least survived. To them it was still a sport, not a scramble for money, or payoffs, or rankings. It was just plain boxing, the manly art of self-defense.

As I ducked through the ropes, I saw my two conspirators ringside. When they saw me looking at them, they turned away, denying me even that elemental kinship.

Joe West still thought this was the night. He talked of other fights and bigger and better things. A title fight with Carlos Monzon if I won.

"Shake my hand and take care a business," Joe West said at the bell.

I didn't dare look at his eyes.

The first four rounds were sick. I danced around, making myself available for punches that would hit me but not hard. I lost all four rounds by a wide margin. I was embarrassingly bad, humiliating both Joe and myself, betraying every moment of the two years we had spent together.

After the fifth round, Joe West slid the stool between the ropes and glared into my face. His eyes were daggers, stabbing into my soul. "I dunno what the fuck yah think yer doin' here, but if yah don't change it I'm gonna walk out!"

"What are you talking about?" I said, spitting to the side.

"I'm sayin' that if yah don't start fightin' this son of a bitch, I'm leavin', walkin' right outta here."

"Bullshit," I said. "You wouldn't do that."

"You know me better 'n that," he warned.

"Okay, I'll see what I can do. Just stay here, huh? Don't leave now . . ."

Joe West nodded seriously. "Now fight this turkey."

I walked out a different person. I started taking the fight to Fourie more, ducking fast and countering with punches to his head and eyes. I wanted to get to those eyes so bad now that I could have spit at them.

I lost the fight by a decision, but Joe West was happier than I thought he'd be. "Man, yah won four outta the last five rounds. Why couldn't yah have jus' fought 'em like that earlier?"

I still could not tell him the truth.

My father met me at the airport when Joe and I returned to Seattle and drove me home. It was a ride surrounded with thick silence, until I told him I might have just fixed a fight. He didn't quite understand what I was talking about, and I tried to explain it more fully.

"Did Joe know what was going on?" he asked.

I shook my head that he didn't. "I'm not sure I really did."

Finally, he said, "Well, you better get out of it then. These things have a way of eating at you and getting worse before they get better."

So I got out of it for a month. But the fact that it was eating at me made me want to get back into it. I returned to the gym and Joe West was happy that I did.

"We gotta lot a offers to go a lot a places," he said. "But I want t'see yah in here workin' hard first. I want yah t'be right in yer head before we hit the road again."

"Why can't we just fight in Seattle?" I asked him again.

He grimaced and shook his head. "I get tired a tryin' to strong-arm my way through the bunch that control boxin' in this town. They all wrapped in t'gether. The commissioners, the promoters, the managers. They throw roadblocks every which a'way. These are the same people that call me a nigger son of a bitch."

"Well, fight them then, Joe. Jesus, have a fight of your own."

Again he would shake his head, but more emphatically. "My dad tried t'fight 'em, an' the government, too. They killed 'em. It jus' can't be done unless I strong-arm my way through. An' shit, man . . . I ain't no kid any more. Yer just about all I got."

But I told him I meant what I said about fighting in Seattle. That led us to discuss setting up Joe West promoting my fights. On paper someone else would have to manage me but Joe would still be calling the shots.

So I started training hard in the gym again, adopting my old fight habits and making a fight a fight. Every thought and action was again directed into prizefighting. It felt good to have a solid idea going once more. It made the shadowy events of Edmonton, Paris, Africa, and Italy recede into the background.

I was just sitting down for a sumptuous Thanksgiving dinner with my family when Joe screeched down their driveway and burst into our house, wearing a grin from ear to ear. "Society," he announced in front of my startled family, "we got it. The champ—Carlos Monzon in Buenos Aires. This is a hell of a break," he said, with unmistakable fervor. "We're goin' t'Argentina inna couple a days."

My family seemed quite happy for me. Everyone, that is, except my father. He stood off in the corner and said nothing. Could he have guessed the trouble ahead?

25

DECEMBER 5, 1971
Luna Park Boxing Arena
Buenos Aires

THE BELL RANG for Round One. Carlos Monzon walked directly across the ring at me. He hunched up his shoulders and raised his hands for the on-guard position. Then his hands started bobbing up and down. His eyes never left their target.

I quickly skittered out of my corner to the left. I wanted to avoid his blind rush, knowing that the early moments of a prizefight can become a straitjacket for the remainder of it. If I could make him miss me for awhile, make him move after me, then I had a chance. A prizefighter's chance.

Then his face hardened and function followed form. The stench of smoldering instincts burned deep within his body. They fathered a punch that shot to my face and stung my eye.

I pushed his hand away and nodded out of respect. Each of his movements was a part of a sequence of predatory actions. I would do something, he would respond, and then I would counter. But Monzon was just laying back, waiting for my response. He was a very savvy aggressor, making me throw the exact punch he wanted to counter. He was a malignant beauty.

Quickly then, I bobbed down to my left and coiled my arm for a hook. I exploded out and up with a hard twist of my body to the right. It smashed against his ear. I had aimed for the ear because I know that if I hit a man there enough, it would upset his balance.

Monzon caught my hook and didn't change expression. Rather, he countered hard and fast with a right hand to my temple. It was a punch that I marveled at, one his body had lied to me about. His feet were cockeyed and he didn't look set for it. I threw my arms across my face and ducked away.

Monzon kept moving forward. He'd jab and I'd counter with left hooks. He'd throw a right, and I'd slap it away, changing the direction of my flight, moving in and out of patterns I hoped he wouldn't diagnose.

Fighting Carlos Monzon was to be my big break. This was going to be the fight to erase all that had happened to me. But it was really to become the turning point, that dead-end street, where I would either turn around and go back, or beat my head against the wall so many times I would become dizzy and sick. It was a chance at fleeting respect, and one I thought would be different.

"We're gonna make this one for the title," I heard Joe West say.

I kept my eyes closed and shifted around in the narrow plane seat. I was in the middle of a great dream. The fight with the world champion had been a tough one, and when they raised my hand and the people surrounded me and screamed congratulations, Joe West began yelling, "We're claimin' the title! We're claimin' the title."

"We're gonna claim the title," Joe West said, nudging me in the ribs. "That's why I want yah under 160, the middleweight limit."

I opened one eye and saw Joe West looking at my face.

"Can't do that," I said. "It's only ten rounds, a nontitle fight."
I yawned and opened both eyes.

"Don't make no difference," he said excitedly. Maybe he
was seeing and feeling the power of my dream. "We're gonna
claim it, champ."

Then the bilingual NO SMOKING and FASTEN SEATBELT signs
flicked on, and Joe West snubbed his cigarette out, clicking
his lap belt together. I looked out the window. We were
descending.

"What were yah weighin' when we left Seattle?" Joe West
asked me.

"One sixty-two."

"Good. I wanna see yah under that limit . . . claim the
title."

"It's a nontitle fight," I said sitting up straight. "But I'm
going to be under 160 anyway. From what I've seen of this
Monzon, I think I can outhustle him. He looks slow to me."

Joe West winked. "He is. You wanna jab and move this
guy. An' when yah stop an' hit 'em, yah wanna hit 'em three
times before yah move away."

I felt the landing gear groan down. Moments later we
were on the ground. The long flight from Seattle to New
York, New York to Rio de Janeiro to Buenos Aires was over.
Fifteen agonizing hours pinched between two armrests that
allowed neither movement nor comfort. But the preflight
excitement of my early days was back so I didn't care.

A slightly built man with soft-boiled eggs for eyes and a
pallid complexion met us at the airport. In a thick British
accent he introduced himself as Mr. Krapper. He was going
to take us to the hotel.

After a long drive, we entered Buenos Aires, a sprawling
city with dark and stodgy buildings shaped like gigantic
boxes. Seeking to hold everything together, were large
courtyards and wide and flat streets. You could look down
the streets until all you could see was the horizon.

Krapper deposited us at an undistinguished hotel on a wide main street. The bags were taken to the second floor room, and after a nap Joe and I asked the middle-aged woman at the desk where we could get a bite to eat. She pointed to a place across the street where large golden chickens sizzled on spits in the window.

"Gimme a steak," Joe West ordered. I asked for the same. He raised his eyebrows. "No more health food?"

"Naw. I want animal meanness for this one," I snarled. That made Joe happy until the waiter explained that they couldn't serve any steak this week, something to do with local politics. He said that there were alternate weeks of fowl and beef.

"How can a fighter be a fighter without beef?" Joe West pondered out loud. I shrugged and we settled on a chicken with mineral water. When it was ordered, Joe West started chuckling. He ripped off a drumstick and held it in front of his mouth.

"That Krapper's something else," he laughed again before biting into it.

"Why's that?"

"No sooner had he got me alone, he tried to place a bet with me."

I cringed a little. "On what?"

"What'a yah think? The fight."

"How much?"

"Five hunnert." Joe West smacked his lips. "Good chicken. Go ahead, eat."

"Well, did you take the bet?" I didn't want to ask but had to.

Joe West watched me. "I don't bet on no prizefights."

I paused before asking the next question. I sliced off a piece of white meat, and held it on my fork. "Well, what was the bet?"

"That you wouldn't win, wouldn't go ten," he replied matter-of-factly.

I moved around in my chair and looked away. I breathed deeply and let it out and looked back to Joe West chewing his drumstick. "Not even your own prizefighter?"

"What?"

"You don't even bet on your own prizefighter?"

Now he hesitated before answering. "I don't bet on prize-fights, period."

I felt a little miffed. If he wouldn't bet on me, did he think I was going to lose? What reason was there then? Surely not the money, it wasn't that much. I thought quickly. Same old story? Same old nonsense?

"What was this guy Krapper like?" I then asked.

He raised his shoulders and let them freeze. "A nice guy. Runs a travel agency down here. I guess he imports the fighters for the main man."

"Who's that?"

"Guy named Tito. They say he's quite a man. He's young and owns the arena, controls Monzon, and is Mister Boxing in these parts."

I studied Joe's face. It was the same face I had seen when we first met six years ago, but it was no longer that friendly. I started to feel manipulated again. Every time he'd talk now it sounded multidimensional. I shook my ideas away, finished my chicken and drank my water. I refused to be bothered by my small hangups now. I had a fight with the middleweight champion of the world in a week and I felt I had better start concentrating on it.

"Everything straight for roadwork and the gym tomorrow?" I asked.

Joe West nodded. "Krapper set it all up. The driver'll be at the hotel inna mornin'. I told 'em seven o'clock."

Joe paid our tab and we went outside. Just before entering the hotel again, a convoy of police vans rumbled down the streets. One of them pulled over to the corner and parked. Then a half a dozen high-booted, uniformed men armed with submachine guns jumped out and stood on the streets, watching everyone.

"On the road again," Joe West said in amazement. "Yah don't see that inna States. Looks like they mean business."

I nodded. "Yeah."

Joe West stared at them. "Reminds me a when I was down in Watts with a prizefighter at Jake's gym. He started some shit with one a the police. It was all I could do t'keep 'em outta jail." Then he grunted once and shook his head even more. "Life is real cheap down here. They'd jus' as soon pull that trigger as stand there."

26

Friendly People

THERE WAS A LOT OF MOVEMENT then; a flurry of arms, glimpses of the referees, the whizzing by colors of the arena. A prizefighter embroiled in a battle doesn't have the opportunity to see much about him. Everything seems to fuse together in one crazy and tilted rainbow.

But there are exceptions. In the clinches, ports in the storm, you can see things. Or even as you are fighting you can spot something, if you're looking for it, if you know it will be there.

I reached out to Monzon, trying to grab at his arms, trying to pull into a clinch. I had to see if a man in sunglasses was at the fight. He said he would be, and I thought I saw him as I entered the arena. But so many tricks had been played on me that I wanted to make sure.

"Grab his elbows," I remember Joe West telling me once. "That takes away their power."

I grabbed Monzon hard and tried to stop him from clubbing the back of my head with his fist. I listened to the crowd, trying to draw energy from them. Then I spotted the man in sunglasses. I almost relaxed. He stood there impassively, nodding to a friend, watching me closely.

But then Monzon pushed me away and smashed my nose. He must have known that nose hits are the worst thing for a fighter to absorb. They rupture tear ducts and make the eyes water. Then the nose bleeds, and is splattered down the chest with each breath. It makes you understand your own mortality.

I moved away from Monzon and thought about the man in the audience. He had met me the second day in Buenos Aires. I remembered he told me he was a reporter. Closer inspection revealed his suit was much too expensive to belong to a man who eked out a living writing witty things under the pressure of a deadline.

I met him one morning after my roadwork as I sat sipping iced tea in a darkened cafe.

"May I sit down?" he asked.

I offered him a chair grudgingly. I didn't want to talk about the fight. It always seemed the more I talked about a fight, the less I wanted to fight it.

"How are you?" he asked easily.

"Fine, it was a good flight. And I really like the city." Stock answers that demanded nothing of me.

He raised the corners of his mouth and looked away to the side. Returning his face to me, he asked, "How do you feel about the fight?"

I nodded. "Good, real good. I think I can win it."

"Do you really? . . ."

I was surprised at his response. "Well, I wouldn't be here . . ."

"If the other fighter hadn't have been taken ill," he interrupted quickly. "Didn't you know that you are nothing but a last-minute substitute?" He seemed desperate.

I shrugged. "It never really concerned me. I don't care about anything but fighting Monzon."

He "smiled" again and scratched his nose nervously. "I'm interested in talking about the fight. You know Carlos Monzon is a stiff puncher?" I said I did. "And you also understand that you didn't win many fights last year?"

"I won some," I said in defense of myself. I didn't like the way the conversation was going.

"You have fought in many places," he said, lowering his voice as the waiter passed by. Then he moved forward in the chair and folded his hands. "Would you still like to fight in a lot of places?"

I stared at him. "If I beat Monzon I can fight anywhere I want."

He smiled briefly and looked away again, lowering his voice. "If you work with us. There is a lot of money bet for Saturday night. . . . The bet is for the fight not to go three rounds. You can even win it if you like, frankly. But only in two rounds. The bell for the third round will not ring."

I breathed deeply and shook my head. There was no oxygen in the room. I kept shaking my head and telling myself to get away. I then shoved my salad aside and reached for my coat, ignoring the man that sat directly across from me.

"You had better listen," he said to me seriously, preventing my arm from touching my coat.

"Screw all your bullshit," I said, drawing away.

"Just listen," the man in the sunglasses said. "You will receive a T-shirt at the gym today, all of the fighters get them. When you get it, wear it. That will mean you are working with us. If you want to bet on the fight, we will cover as much money as you would like. But the bet is that it doesn't go three rounds."

I stared hard at him. "There will be a lot more places and fights, too, and some you will win." He meant business.

"You have all week," he added. "We'll be watching you carefully." Then he smiled. "It doesn't make sense to create trouble for yourself, frankly. Merely wear the shirt and you will be taken care of."

Then he leaned over even farther and dropped his voice to its lowest octave. "Wear that shirt, or there will be trouble. We don't have time to postpone what has already been done."

I couldn't talk and he quickly rose out of his seat, grabbing my hand and shaking it. "Thank you," he said, pumping it. "Thank you very much."

I sat there and watched him leave. Then I bolted to the door after him. "Wait a minute . . ." I said. The street was nearly empty, save for a toothless old woman who lifted a large metal cup into my face and shook it, begging for money. I asked her in rapid Spanish where the two men had gone. She grinned wretchedly and shook the cup again. "Aw, fuck it!" I said, snapping my arms down. I walked back into the restaurant.

And what's this shit about the T-shirt? And other fights and other places? Jesus, I thought. They really came at me quick. But he said he didn't have much time, didn't he. He said I was really a substitute for someone else.

I chuckled nervously. "I'll bet they're really sweating it," I said out loud to no one. This time I had to tell Joe. "No," I then said just as quickly. "Get my own knack of survival."

Before stepping into the street again, I paused in the doorway of the restaurant and looked both ways. Then I crossed the street and returned quickly to the hotel, with a feeling of total isolation. Once there, I stewed about the whole prizefight scene again. Somehow, I started to blame Joe West. I sat and listened to country western music until Joe came and got me for the gym.

"You were gone a long time," he said, checking his watch. "Where'd yah go?"

I stared at him, at his smile, his nice clothes, and the gym bag that he held. "What do you mean where did I go?" I snapped.

Joe West pulled his head back and raised his eyebrows.

"It's a simple question, man. I'm not tryin' t'pry into yer precious time," he answered sarcastically.

I apologized and said I was getting uptight about a lot of things. Joe just grinned and snapped his fingers. "That's good. Yah should be that way. I know yer ready t'fight when yah get jumpy. Now c'mon, we gotta meet the driver downstairs."

I walked with him and thought of the man in the sunglasses and what he said. It was something about getting a T-shirt today at the gym. I was supposed to wear it and that would mean I was working with them. Preposterous.

Upon arrival at the gym, I got out of the car slowly, gazing around and looking for faces with sunglasses. A small crowd met us outside and led us to the gym. Where was the T-shirt? I asked myself as introductions were made.

After a good workout and shower, we stood around again for more introductions and pictures. But there was no T-shirt. I breathed a sigh of relief as we finally were taken back to the hotel.

"Good work today," Joe said.

I agreed. "Yeah, I'm loosening up." They were bluffing I said to myself happily.

"How's the weight?"

"I checked it after I showered. One fifty-nine on the button."

"Yah got four more days a trainin'," Joe West advised. "That's plenty a time, I don't wanna see yah down around 157 too early."

"No problem," I said. I believed there would be no problems. I was again on the upswing of the roller coaster ride, in a car manned by Joe West.

27

The Shirt

I watched Carlos Monzon closely. He moved around me in ever diminishing circles, like a vulture waiting for the kill, patiently picking its moments to strike. Three rounds, the man in sunglasses had told me. It wasn't supposed to go three. I laughed cryptically and threw a hard jab and crossed with my own right hand. They were partially deflected as Monzon covered up.

When I hadn't received that shirt, I was ecstatic, thinking again, like in South Africa, that the men were bluffing and merely trying to mess with my mind. I felt strong again, and formed a new resolve about prizefighting.

I knew I had been foolish to blame Joe for everything. I was the one who wanted to hit the road, instead of staying in college and surrounding myself with an easier life. I was the one who wanted something different. But it was on the road that I had lost my identity. I struggled with a middle-class background, and its mores and ethics. I wanted desperately to be from the road like Joe West and at the same time to love it, relish it, to be able to talk fast and free. The road had prompted Joe and I to bump heads. It was only natural. He was fifty and black, and I barely old enough to vote and white. I needed friends that I could talk to instead of the isolated feeling I encountered amidst ten thousand people.

"Everything meaningful is a struggle," Joe West had once told me. "Marriage, relationships, you and I . . . Sure we've had our troubles, but we can work it out."

I felt confident again. I wasn't ever going to let anybody tell me what to do. I bounced away from Monzon as he huffed and puffed after me. I was doing exactly what I should have been doing. I was tactics and strategy, making him move after me, side to side, jabbing and crossing with right hands when he didn't expect them. And I saw Joe West in the corner, happy.

"That's it, Society!" I could almost hear him scream like he had done before. "Now yah got 'em." Moving around the ring with a clear head was as easy as morning roadwork. It was a feeling that had been missing for too long a time.

I was shaving in front of the bathroom mirror after a good early morning run when I first started to make a series of meaningless stands. Joe came into my room and stood at the bathroom door and watched me.

"How's roadwork?" he asked.

"Good," I said. "It's a nice place to run."

He coughed and cleared his throat. "Yah know they won't let yah fight with yer moustache down here."

"Who won't?" I scoffed, glancing at Joe West.

"The commission. They say if yah get cut onna mouth, their doctors couldn't work on it right."

"Mouth cut?" I said incredulously.

Joe West snickered. "Yeah, I agree. It's a little silly."

"So?"

"Cut it off."

I shook my head and patted my face with a towel. "Not today. Let them worry about it for a while."

Joe and I had breakfast and mapped out more tactics. "He's a puncher, an' that's it," Joe said over coffee. "Now yah gotta move t'each side a him. Remember 'em like a train onna track. Don't stand in front of it, get t'the side."

"Right," I said. "And he's easy to hit with overhand rights, too."

Joe West winked. "That's right. Take a quick step t'the right when he jabs, an' then toss that overhand right. We'll work on it inna gym today, on the bag."

"No, let me spar. I'm sure they have a guy around to spar with."

"Yeah, he's short and fast, the opposite of Monzon," he said. "But man, yah in good shape as it is. Yah musta boxed close t'two hunnert rounds in Seattle gettin' ready."

"But I didn't know I'd be fighting the middleweight champion of the world."

"It's just somethin' t'call oneself," Joe replied. "He ain't the best I've seen."

"He's still the champion."

"Ah, forget about that. Now one other thing yah gotta do with this guy is when yah get inna clinch, grab his elbows. Yah know he's gonna be clubbin' at yah with the right hand in 'em."

I shook my head once. "I know, I just don't see how they can get away with that. It's illegal."

"A lotta things are," Joe West said seriously. Then he snapped out of it and became excited again. "Yah see, man, everybody's got defeat in 'em. What yah gotta do is bring it outta 'em. An' the best way t'do that is to take away what he does best. Monzon'll try t'club yah. Don't let 'em work on yah inna clinches. Make 'em messed up and desperate. When he gets that way he'll get careless. When he gets careless then, he'll lose."

I wondered whether Joe really knew who he was talking about.

That afternoon we went to the gymnasium again. When we got through the doors, I was surrounded by a bunch of people who wanted autographs and handshakes. Joe West moved through the crowd and walked over to a man who stood watching me with his arms folded. Joe motioned me over.

"This is Tito," he said.

Tito offered a lazy smile and shook my hand. He was tall, trim, and well-dressed. I didn't go for the hair grease he favored, though.

"We can't get any steak around here," Joe said.

"I have steak," Tito said through his pleasant smile. His dark brown eyes enjoyed staring at Joe West, who was now falling into his prim and proper speech habits.

All of a sudden, Tito lifted something up and handed it to me. It was the T-shirt. I stared at it. "I hope you enjoy . . . your stay in Buenos Aires," he said.

The fish had been baited. I took the shirt. Joe and I walked into the dressing room and proceeded to get ready. I could do nothing but think about the shirt, and Tito's connection to it. Probably nothing, I said. Shit, those men probably know that the visiting fighters always get a shirt for advertisement.

"C'mon, get goin'," Joe said, checking his watch.

He was right, I was stalling. I sat on the chair, shirtless, with everything ready to go out and spar. "Here," Joe West said, picking up the shirt and tossing it to me.

I jumped to the side, letting it hit the floor in a muffled plop. It raised the dust in the corner of the room. "No, let's wear one of our own, okay?"

Joe West walked to the T-shirt and lifted it up and spread it out. It had blazoned across the front of it "Luna Park," set against a backdrop of the northern and southern hemisphere, with two fighters going at it.

"If a guy is nice enough t'give yah a present, I think yah oughta wear it," Joe said.

I shook my head and slipped my own over my head and shoulders. It had my name on the back of it and it felt good on. "Let's save it for another time. It's too good a shirt to wreck in the gym."

Joe West folded it up and laid it in the bag. I was now happy. I had made a stand, refusing to go along with all the bullshit.

When we returned to the hotel, Joe and I began talking about prizefighting seriously.

"You know, we've been pretty successful at this," I said. "If you look at the overall record."

Joe West agreed. "Yah can never be really successful at it, yah can't afford t'look at it that way. The success has t'be a dream that yah keep shootin' for. If yah think yah got it, then yer likely t'wind up inna nightmare. That's why I didn't want yah t'quit after the Benvenuti thing. They stole it from yah, an' quittin' woulda jus' been admittin' that one bit a success. But this here fight'll make it all return. The more I think about it, the better I like it."

"Yeah, but after really winning it, and they stopped it, I just didn't feel there was any point to it any more."

I felt I was getting in the mood of talking with Joe West again. We hadn't really been close since Italy, or even since New York when we signed to fight for the title.

"Well," Joe said. "You were jus' a kid then. You've grown up a hell of a lot. But yah wanna always keep boxin' inna dream state. I know we've been through some shitty deals, but that can all change here. I'm really countin' on yah in this one."

That was it, I told myself. I wasn't going to let anything bother me. Everything I heard about deals was going to be forgotten. I could tell from Joe's face that he was counting on me again. And Jesus, I was twenty-three years old now. If I can't fend for myself now, then when?

"I feel good, Joe," I said as I looked away. "You won't be disappointed."

I did roadwork the next morning in the usual place, and returned to the hotel to have breakfast with Joe. We talked more tactics and confidence. I ate a full breakfast, so Joe West said, "Yah better go an' walk that meal down. Yah don't want it t'lump up in yer stomach."

"Right," I said.

When I hit the streets, I stayed away from the restaurant the two men had approached me in. But at every street corner I would pause and slowly look about me. They had said they were going to be following me, and if any of their words were true, they would know by now that I hadn't worn their T-shirt.

As I walked swiftly through the streets, I would imagine every one approaching as an opponent. I would bob my shoulders down, seeing a punch coming, and then counter. I twitched every muscle in my neck and arms that would simulate the punch.

Bobbing and weaving through the crowd then, I spied the light about to change and stop pedestrian traffic. I thought of Joe West's old story about the prizefighter who believed that if he missed a traffic light he would lose the fight. I shot ahead with the same idea.

In my haste, I bumped into an old man and he tumbled to the ground. Everyone stared at me, so I stooped over to help him up. "Damn," I said. "I missed the light."

I helped him up and stood on the street corner, feeling the breeze as the cars rolled past. "Signs are adjustable," I said to myself, again mimicking Joe West's words.

Then I felt something press sharply into my lower back. I glanced around to my left quickly to tell someone to quit pushing, and I saw the man with the sunglasses. He had his hands in his pocket and pressed forward into my back.

"The shirt, punk. Get the shirt from the nigger and wear it! Three rounds, we're watching."

Then he gave me a shove and I landed in the street. An oncoming car screeched to a stop just to the right of me and the driver shook a fist and yelled out his window.

I jumped back on the sidewalk and spun all the way around, looking for the man. I thought I saw him crossing the street. Then people started pushing past me. I was so scared that I couldn't talk.

I returned to the hotel quickly. The lady at the desk asked me if the reporters had found me. "Reporters?" I asked. She nodded and said two men asked where I was. She said she told them I was out of the hotel.

I couldn't find Joe West now and I felt desperate. Because I couldn't, I felt he had deserted me. I needed help, but he had told me I was grown up. Would I be less than that if I asked for help?

I wore the T-shirt that afternoon and every day after. I began to spend more time in my room until I simply refused to go out of it. I began to connect everything about past fights again, and then blamed Joe West. I didn't want to come here in the first place. He made me. He made me become a prizefighter. He took me on the road, when I wanted to stay in Seattle. He this, he that . . . I felt I was going nuts.

At dinner that night I ate like a frightened pig. It didn't go unnoticed by Joe West. I tried hard to hold onto my act.

"How was yer weight this afternoon at the gym?"

I shrugged. "Good."

He looked away. "I saw yah eatin' good this mornin', too."

"I was hungry."

"Yah worried about the fight? Yah shouldn't be, it's jus' a fight."

I looked up from my plate. "What do you mean?"

"Martha eats when she's worried."

"I was just hungry. You said you wanted me to eat."

"But all that bread an' butter?"

"Will you forget about it? I'm alright."

He nodded and lit a cigarette. "I know yah are . . ."

28

Decision

I WANTED DESPERATELY to talk honestly with Joe West. I knew he was my only friend among the faceless, that his voice, barely heard through the din, was soothing. But I was grown-up now and was expected to fend for myself.

I had one recourse open to me. I tried to recapture the feeling I had when I fought Nino Benvenuti for his title in Italy. If ever I was ready for a fight, it was that one. I replayed everything that led up to it, everything that I did to get so ready. And then I hit upon the prostitutes that had visited me before the fight and the weigh-in. They had made me powerful and cold, I recalled. They had made me hate myself to a point where I was comfortable in the knowledge that I would DIE before I would lose the fight.

So the night before fighting Carlos Monzon, I was on the streets again. I looked for two legs that could flash me back to a point where everything wasn't so confused and frightening. I found her outside of a movie theater a few blocks down from the hotel. She was heavy-thighed and homely, but that didn't matter. She held it in her hands and increased it. Everything was quiet as she left, money in hand, and I stood naked, reduced to basic emotions.

The next evening I stood in front of my dresser mirror in my hotel room, wearing sunglasses similar to the man that said he'd be following me. I looked straight into the mirror and screwed up my mouth. My hand formed itself into a gun.

"The fight doesn't go three," the mirrored image said from behind sunglasses.

"Fuck you," I replied.

"We mean it," the mirror said. It then pointed the muzzle of the gun at myself.

"Pull the trigger!" I said. "Life is cheap down here."

"Three rounds."

"Pull it."

"Three."

"Pull!" I said out loud. "Pull!"

There was a knock on my door. "That you, man?"

I peeled off the glasses and opened my hand, unlocking the door. "Yeah. Come in."

Joe West looked around. "I heard yah talkin' in here."

"Just singing a song," I replied. Joe said it was time to go.

Luna Park Arena stood at the end of a long road that cut through the middle of Buenos Aires. It was close to the harbor and I could smell the sea. The arena itself looked old and used, like an artist's studio that cranked out many cheap paintings for every masterpiece.

"This way," Joe West said, following an usher.

The place was now empty, and eerie to walk through. We passed the darkened ring and it looked to be a monument to some futile idea I once had. The usher led us to the last dressing room on the left down a long, rectangular corridor. Every dressing room I'd been in was for some reason down such a corridor.

"It's pink!" Joe West said gazing around, after he pushed open the door. He set everything down and put his hands on his hips. "Now what the fuck kinda color is that for a dressin' room." It was the same color pink as the first Los Angeles hotel I had stayed in.

Then the promoter came to our room and seemed intent on making everything right for us. Everyone wished each other luck and left. I sat on a table and stared at Joe West preparing everything. There was a lot of noise now, coming from outside the door.

"Will you close that fucking door," I blurted out.

Joe West swung around and looked at me with a cigarette dangling from his bottom lip. He walked over and slammed it.

I kept thinking of so many things that I couldn't think at all. I was close to catatonic. When Joe returned to his table, a short, profusely sweating, dark-skinned man burst through the door. He asked Joe West for some tape.

"What's he want?" Joe West asked me, not understanding what the man was asking for.

I pointed to the tape. "These fuckers call themselves managers . . ." Joe West muttered, handing him a full roll and escorting him out. "They have the gall t'ask me for tape."

The din from the full arena told me the fights were starting now. Joe West wrapped my hands and I prepared myself.

"We're on," Joe West finally said, moving quickly through the door. He snuffed out a cigarette and gathered the fight gear in a small bag. "They got a TV camera at the end a the hall. They wanna talk t'yah."

I was cold. I wrapped my robe around me and it stuck to all the Vaseline that covered my chest. My mouth was dry and I tried to spit, only to have it hang on my lip and drip down my face. Joe West stood at the door and motioned me out.

When I walked around the door I saw the cameras at the end of the hall. Bright lights were pointed toward me. I walked past other dressing rooms; fighters who had already fought sticking their heads out to watch me. At the end of the hall a crowd of people now gathered watching me walk toward them. Nothing but faces. I thought I saw sunglasses.

The TV announcer stopped me and asked me what I was thinking. I turned to him and said, "Solo se que no se nada." It was an old Spanish phrase I had learned some nine years ago in junior high.

The announcer looked shocked for a moment, and then spun quickly to his audience, telling them that it was the old Socratic statement saying, "I only know that I know nothing."

"Let's get t'the ring," Joe said.

We walked down a pathway with anxious looking people on each side. They bent over, through the guards and walked with me, and tried to pound my back.

"What are yah lookin' at," Joe West asked, noticing that I scanned the crowd.

I thought I saw another pair of sunglasses. "Nothing," I answered.

29

"Nada, Nada"

As I SPUN AWAY again from Carlos Monzon, I spied the man in the sunglasses. It's him, the real one, I said to myself.

"The fight doesn't go three rounds."

Monzon then jabbed with a long left hand and sneaked a right hand in behind it. It smashed into my side and I gasped for breath.

"Take care a business!" I thought I heard Joe West say.

The round was almost over, I said to myself. Then the bell rang and I grabbed my side. Joe West was already in the ring, helping me to my corner. "What's wrong with yah side?"

"I broke it," I grimaced, sitting uneasily on my stool. I glanced around quickly and the arena's eyes watched my every move.

Joe West rubbed my rib cage and looked beaten. "Can yah go another?"

I twisted my head once and said I didn't know.

"Yah got to 'em good out there," Joe West said soothingly. "Yah got that left hook workin'."

I looked up into his eyes. "Yeah?"

He nodded quickly. "I think yah can take this dude . . ."

I sat impassively on the stool.

"Well, can yah go another?"

I tightened my jaw around my mouthpiece and heard the buzzer alerting the corner men that they had to exit the ring. "Get out," I said to Joe West.

"Yah gonna go another?" Joe West said at the bell, wanting to stand by me until I was sure. "Yer movin' 'em good." I thought quickly and nodded and then stood up and walked out for a fight. I was getting to him. Every punch I threw hit him. Every time I wanted to get away, I could.

"Fight 'em, man!" I heard Joe West say as he took his perch at ringside again.

Monzon came at me with a deranged, soul-splitting look. He went directly to work on my side. When I covered it, he changed strategy. He hit my arms, and then my head, and made me want to cover up in so many places I would have had to have been an octopus.

I grabbed him hard, trying to stifle his action, but he was stronger both mentally and physically than I. In the clinches he clubbed my head until it felt like a drum. From outside of the ring I heard Joe West.

"Goddammit! Move! Speed and movement!"

I then started swinging at Monzon with everything that I had left. A few lefts and a few rights. He was all over me, blocking punches, absorbing others, and countering like a master.

I know all of those moves, I said to myself. Why can't I do that?

Another jab and right hand found me vulnerable. Where is he? I asked myself. I glanced at the crowd. When I needed the man in the sunglasses for an excuse, I couldn't find him.

I glanced out at the crowd again in desperation. I had to know if the man in sunglasses was there. Carlos Monzon still wasn't giving me the time I needed. He slammed another right hand to my gut. I breathed hard and wondered when the bell would ring.

Then the bell rang, and I spun around to walk to my corner. I spied the sunglasses and grabbed my side again and sat down. Joe West jumped through the ropes and knelt over. "How's it?"

I soured up my face and didn't answer.

Joe West ran his hand across my side and said, "It doesn't look hurt."

I stared at him. I didn't know what to say. I kept the pained look on my face and touched it, slightly bending over. I saw more faces join Joe West. One belonged to a doctor, one was the referee's. The rest were faces of my friends and family and everyone I had ever fought with. Benvenuti was there, the Mexican that I fought in Edmonton. And then they were joined by the Frenchman, and then the South African. Then they all had sunglasses on. I knew I was going crazy.

"How is it?" Joe West demanded. "It doesn't look hurt!"

I lifted my head up and blinked my eyes trying to hold back the tears. "It doesn't have to have blood on it to be hurt," I answered. Joe West paused for a moment and looked deep into my eyes accusingly. But what could he say? He had used the very words in Paris.

"Can yah go another?" Joe West asked me harshly. More faces joined in my corner.

I blinked rapidly, tasting the poison in my mouth. "No!" I whispered hoarsely. "It's killing me."

That was it. I now had lied to Joe West like I never had lied before. The other lies could be called courageous, as I tried to fend for myself. But this was a dark and ugly one, a lie from a coward who refused to fight any longer.

I heard the bell ring and saw Monzon stand up and approach me. People then started waving their arms and screaming. Monzon had won.

Joe West was emotionless now. It was as if he knew his prizefighter had just bagged out. I found it hard to face him. He led me back to the dressing room slowly.

I sat on the table and a doctor tore off tape from a tick roll and pasted it to my side. The promoter came in to see if I was alright. I said I was. Then he asked me if I wanted an X-ray of it. I thought quickly. An X-ray? An X-ray? Of course! That would show that absolutely nothing was wrong with my side, that I was forced to quit by threats and men flexing muscles that had nothing to do with a prizefight.

"Yes," I said. "Let's get it X-rayed."

Then Joe West leaned over and whispered, "Yah better keep grabbin' that side. If they think yah jus' quit, they won't pay yah."

I snapped my head around to Joe's face. What is he talking about? Does he already know what I did? "What do you mean?" I asked, grabbing my side again.

He ignored me and then flashed me a look. I knew damn well what he meant.

He thinks I just quit! I said to myself. Then I sobered, Why shouldn't he think that? I did. This was the moment I felt anything that those two men could have done to me couldn't equal the hurt reflected in Joe West's eyes. I felt close to standing up and telling everyone what happened. But the words that flashed in my head in explanation sounded empty, and were those of a loser. No, not a loser but a quitter. Professional sports can stand a few losers, but not quitters. When the public pays for something, they deserve to get what they pay for.

They didn't get it tonight. Only two men were satisfied. Maybe a half a dozen, maybe more. Everyone connected to the gambit of betting on a scripted prizefight such as this one had to be satisfied. They were the only ones that could still count the money in their pocket.

"Let's get it X-rayed, okay?" I said again.

After the pictures at the doctor's they had us wait in the reception room. Joe West furtively smoked cigarette after cigarette and refused to look at me. The promoter was there, too.

We all heard footsteps then coming down the hall. Everyone's eyes looked toward the manila envelope the doctor gave to the promoter. "Nada, nada," he said.

30

Back Home Again

BEING IN SEATTLE again made everything worse. I had to keep to the story that I had injured my side in the fight. I felt a responsibility to conceal what I had done. I even stayed away from the restaurant for a couple of days. I knew that if Mike and Rich asked me about the fight I couldn't lie to them. They were the only friends that I had that weren't concerned about sports and prizefighting. They never really cared whether I won or lost.

I finally showed up there and as expected they asked me about it. I started telling them that I was winning the fight until the injury, and then finally just reached the end of the excuses. They saw that I was really disturbed about something and wanted to know exactly what the matter was.

"My side's alright," I said, shaking my head and pounding it with my fist. I tried to take the hate I was feeling for myself out of my side.

"What do you mean?" Mike asked.

"I took a dive."

Mike and Rich looked at each other. "No . . ."

"Yes. Remember those other things that I told you about in prizefighting?"

"You mean about the name changes and stuff?" Rich asked.

I nodded. "Well, this one was worse." And then I told them all about it, plus the whole scene in South Africa. They couldn't believe it.

"I can't believe it either," I said. "I've never felt so low in my life."

"You're locked in now," Rich then nodded. "There's nothing you can do but quit."

I shook my head tiredly. "I can't quit. I want to help Joe West get established as a promoter in this town. He can't do it without me."

"You have to quit," Mike said seriously. "This is the type of thing that can get you in big trouble. These sound like heavyweight people."

I nodded that they were. "But Seattle's different. I don't have to deal with anyone else in this town. The deals out of the country were different."

"There's a real fine line between the two," Rich added. "What about all those fighters around here that change their names."

"Yeah," Mike chimed in. "Remember when you fought Moyer the second time? You told us then that one of the fights that night was fixed. What's the difference?"

I shrugged, not really knowing. "But that was secondhand info. Something I just heard. I've never really been approached in this town."

"What about when you were approached to fight that guy in the Coliseum? Were you to win the first, lose the second, and then really fight the third?"

"But I don't know if the guy was kidding or not," I said. "I thought he was . . ."

"Maybe you better start thinking different," Rich said.

"What, expose myself so I can be free?" I laughed hollowly, sarcastically. "No, I'm just going to go back to the gym and fight a couple of more times, see if I know what to do in a real fight."

I started training again for Joe West. We set up his promotion company, sold part of my contract to a friend of mine in the gym, a tough New Yorker who had been teaching me some things, and set up a fight for March 1, 1972. I won an easy ten-round decision. I thought everything would be relieved after a real fight. I was wrong.

Other fighters began telling me stories about promoters. It was a big joke to them, as if prizefighting were nothing but a carnival, something to entertain the suckers that paid money to see two people fight.

I had started writing things down by now, everything that had happened to me in prizefighting, and on the road. I confided in a few people and wrote a few warmup articles in a local newspaper.

Joe West, meanwhile, had scheduled another fight for me. As I was training for it, I helped him out with some publicity. I was being interviewed in the restaurant about fighting a crosstown pug and I let slip that he had participated, unwittingly, in a fixed fight.

A local television station wanted to interview me.

"Tickets for the fight are goin' aw'right," Joe said. "Oh, and there's gonna be a TV camera here t'watch yah work out. They wanna ask yah about what yah said about that guy's fights bein' fixed."

"All right."

He sucked on his cigarette. "Yah know yah gotta be careful with what yah say. Yah can get in real trouble."

"How?"

"The commission'll make yah talk or they'll bust yah."

"I don't have to talk to them," I said defiantly. "Especially after what they've said about you."

"Oh, they're aw'right," Joe West said. "I can put up with 'em. But when yah talk about that fight fix crap, they can stop my promotions. Yah see, what you do reflects on me."

"Oh shit, Joe. You've heard about fixes . . ."

"Yeah, but havin' facts an' hearin' about it are different things. I jus' know what I hear inna gym."

"Well, I have more than that," I said. I felt real close to spilling the whole thing to Joe.

"Talk ain't shit," Joe West said. "Nobody'd stand with yah when it came right down to it."

"Would you?" I asked, staring at him closely.

He stared at me and then nodded slowly. "Yah know I'd support yah, but you'd need facts. I'm tellin' yah you'd be pissin' in the wind."

"Well, if everyone compared notes then, it would come out."

"That's a dangerous thing," Joe West said, hesitating.

"Maybe some good could come out of it?"

"A lotta hurt, too."

"Well," I said, sitting back down on the bench. "We'll see then."

I got to my feet quickly and glanced around the dressing room at all of the empty T-shirts and head protectors and gloves. There were protective cups laying on the bench, too, seemingly worthless and meaningless unless worn by a prizefighter. So many real things came to life when a prizefighter donned his gear. I grabbed a towel and started walking out. I paused again at the door, where the scales were. I slid the weight bar around for a second and lost myself in thought. I walked out and stepped into the ring and began loosening up.

The sportscaster came in and set up the camera and said hello. My thoughts were still accelerating. Something popped inside of me.

"Keep that fuckin' camera on me," I said to the sports-caster. "I'm going to blow the lid off!"

The announcer asked me a question that he said the com-mission would—did I have knowledge of any fixed fights. I shook all over, and my throat tightened. Then I slowly started shaking my head and said I did. In the following sentence I announced then and there, my retirement from the ring. I just couldn't take it anymore. I knew the commission would suspend me anyway.

The room erupted, Joe West looked at me and cried that I was through. He cried like a man that had been denied his chance, his last chance, to get established in a town that just wouldn't let him operate. And like a man that had been implicated.

I stepped out of the ring and walked down the hall and got into my clothes and left the gym. I was crying the whole time, and felt silly to have tears falling so openly down my cheeks. Me, Mr. Tough Guy.

31

Opening Up

I WAS WALKING NORTH, up Roosevelt Way, the street the restaurant was on. I paused at the door and let the stinging wind burn my face and dry up the tears. I grabbed the door-knob and walked in.

"I just quit," I said to Rich.

He briefly glanced at me and returned to frying up the rice. "Feel better?" His nonchalance surprised me.

I shook my head and looked away. "Worse. I couldn't tell them the whole thing. I just said that I was involved in fixed fights. It was even worse than fixing the fights, Rich," I said, turning and facing him. "I made it sound like Joe West had done it."

"Oh, no," he said, squinting his eyebrows.

Then the telephone began ringing and he walked over to it and said hello. He then just stood there for a few seconds, listening. He crossed his eyebrows and hung it up.

"Who's that?" I asked.

"Somebody threatening to burn down the place," he said. "They said that you were in deep trouble." He thought it over and nodded. "I guess you did really do it."

Rich manned the phone all day, screening my calls. There

were more crank ones, and a few from friends. The word seemed to travel fast. Then the sportscaster called and invited me to be on live television, during their news hour, to further explain what I had said. I agreed, thinking that could be the time to tell it all.

But as I thought about it, it all sounded so crazy. Taken as isolated incidents, the fixes didn't sound credible. I probably couldn't have beaten Carlos Monzon anyway, and how could I go into the things about betting on prizefights I had heard in South Africa? How a bettor can get the odds he wants if he bets on a certain round, and not just the outcome. And how could I say anyone's name? I called my lawyer.

It was odd to talk about something like this with a lawyer. He asked me what I was going to tell. I said I was going to spill it. He then spoke of the lawsuits that could be generated from something like that.

The phone at the restaurant kept ringing and Rich kept answering it. After another crank call, he finally just shook his head and lifted it off the hook. "I'm not listening to that any more," he said. "What the hell have you done?"

I shrugged and drove to the television studio, parking across the street. When I entered it I was led to the main studio where they were preparing for the six o'clock telecast. Then Joe West and my lawyer arrived. He further handcuffed me as he carefully explained libel laws to me. I apologized to Joe West.

I sat in my chair frozen, feeling totally removed from what was happening. Just a few hours ago I was ready to implicate the world and clean up boxing. Now I wanted to just slip quietly away and never be seen again.

When they broke to a commercial and set us at the table in front of the cameras, I felt even sillier, and more confused. I knew what I wanted to do, but felt restrained from doing it. "Nobody would back yah up," I remembered Joe West saying. I felt as alone then as I had never felt in my life.

We came on camera and I lamely apologized to a few people I had unwittingly implicated. As I stared into the camera I saw uncounted thousands of people that really didn't care about prizefighting. I felt like telling them how much I loved it, and how I felt it was being abused by a handful, and by everyone that lets it continue in that manner. I felt though, like I was destroying the very thing that had given me so much life.

After the telecast, we watched a replay of it in the control booth. I looked like that kid pissin' in the wind as Joe West put it. I felt rudderless, like a boat set adrift into a raging current. Everyone else had long bailed out and I stood alone with a spinning wheel in my hand.

We all stood in the studio for a moment, talking to a reporter. Then Joe West and I started walking out.

"That took guts, Society," Joe West said. He then reached into his long leather jacket that he had bought in Italy, and placed a cigarette in his mouth. When he struck the match, its flame flashed red and yellow against his face, like the tail of a comet, before collapsing into smoke.

I shuffled my feet. "You haven't called me Society for a long time."

He glanced at me and nodded once. "Well, like I said, that took guts."

"You want to know what happened?"

He looked away and a passing car's headlights lit up his face. His blue eyes were wet and his moustache seemed to droop more than I had ever seen. Deep lines crossed his forehead. "No, I don't think I do."

I nodded and we both stood still. "Well," Joe West said, offering his hand to me. "I gotta go. Martha'll have dinner waitin'. Yah take care a business, huh?"

I watched him walk away, periodically illuminated by a passing car's headlights. I watched him until I could no longer see anything left on the streets. I then turned quickly and walked to my own car, feeling that at last something had been removed from my life. It gave me a good feeling and an empty one. Though I couldn't erase what the fight game had done to me, I had at least made a first step.

Epilogue

UNDERSTANDABLY, the Washington State Boxing Commission took a dim view of what I had said on television. What I had said reflected on them as much as it did on Joe West. They suspended me and called for a hearing to air out what I had said.

They held the hearing at the Washington State Athletic Headquarters and the room was filled with reporters and television cameras, plus a number of local boxing principals and aficionados.

I still felt in a straitjacket, knowing that I should only try to make clear that I had never participated in a fixed fight in Seattle. My lawyer, Charles Sandell, one of the city's most knowledgeable, advised me of the possibilities of unwittingly or wittingly libeling any one of a number of people, including Joe West.

I told the Commission, since my direct charges did not concern fights in Seattle, that I really had nothing to say. A cop-out, but at this point I was only too aware of "pissin' in the wind." The commissioners then asked me if I would speak to a national boxing body about my charges. I said I would consider it. They then "revealed" that they had brought in a Mr. Bob Turly from California, a World Boxing Council official.

I immediately felt that the Washington State Commission was playing games with me in an effort to save their own necks. I asked Mr. Turly what area he had jurisdiction over. It turned out to be just a few western states, where none of my fixed fights had occurred. Since he had no jurisdiction over places like Paris, Canada, or Buenos Aires, I felt no compunction to speak to him.

During all of this I tried to explain to the commissioners and the press that my feelings were totally on the side of prizefighting, and not against it. I only wanted to throw the rascals out of the fight game.

Shortly thereafter the FBI contacted me and said they were doing an extensive investigation of boxing in the Seattle area. They told me that I could talk to them confidentially. I told them everything I knew—what I had done, what I had heard from other prizefighters, and even scuttlebutt from the hangers-on at the gym. I told them who they should talk to in the area, people who might know more than me. To questions about foreign activity, I only sketched the basic things that had happened.

I was called before a grand jury empaneled to look at boxing fixes in the Seattle area. I again answered all of their questions about the local scene, but balked when the district attorney pressured me to explain everything that had happened overseas and in Canada. My lawyer had told me that though grand jury proceedings are secret, the prosecutor can release anything he wants to make public.

That handcuffed me to a certain extent, though I did briefly touch on some of the things that had happened. I also told them explicitly that I only wanted to get the wrong people out of prizefighting. I was very touchy about that. I didn't want to give anyone the idea that I really disliked the fight game, or that I was simply turning against something that at one time gave me great pleasure.

I told them I was writing this book about my experiences and trying to enlist other people's help in verifying all that I knew was going on. As Joe West had guessed, not too many people were eager to help. The few replies I did receive said they didn't want anything to do with my project. Most said they still had to make their living from prizefighting. That destroyed my idea about writing an investigative book on boxing. So I then made the decision just to write down what had happened to me, to convey generally a feeling of what had gone on behind the scenes.

My purpose in all of this is to make prizefighting a sport worthy of the public that pays to see it. The only way that might happen is for those in the fight game who care to compare notes and inspect what is dredged up. If that doesn't happen, then prizefighting will stay as it has. And that will be a real shame—for the boxers, managers, promoters, and fans. Boxing's pure mystery will continue to take a back seat to one underhanded deal after another.

Index